IN BED WITH WALL STREET

IN BED WITH WALL STREET

THE CONSPIRACY CRIPPLING OUR GLOBAL ECONOMY

LARRY DOYLE

palgrave
macmillan

First published in 2014 by PALGRAVE MACMILLAN® in the U.S.—
a division of St. Martin's Press LLC, 175 Fifth Avenue, New York, NY
10010.

Where this book is distributed in the UK, Europe and the rest of the
world, this is by Palgrave Macmillan, a division of Macmillan Publishers
Limited, registered in England, company number 785998, of Houndmills,
Basingstoke, Hampshire RG21 6XS.

Palgrave Macmillan is the global academic imprint of the above
companies and has companies and representatives throughout the world.

Palgrave® and Macmillan® are registered trademarks in the United States,
the United Kingdom, Europe and other countries.

ISBN: 978-1-137-27872-2

Library of Congress Cataloging-in-Publication Data

Doyle, Larry, 1960–
  In bed with Wall Street : the conspiracy crippling our global economy /
Larry Doyle.
    pages   cm
  ISBN 978-1-137-27872-2 (alk. paper)
  1. Finance—Political aspects—United States. 2. Finance—Government
policy—United States 3. Financial institutions—Corrupt practices—
United States. 4. Monetary policy—United States. 5. United States—
Economic policy. I. Title.
HG181.D69   2014
332.0973—dc23

                                                           2013028220

A catalogue record of the book is available from the British Library.

Design by Letra Libre, Inc.

First edition: January 2014

10 9 8 7 6 5 4 3 2 1

Printed in the United States of America.

CONTENTS

PREFACE

"YOU'RE NOT GOING TO REALLY KNOW ANYTHING FOR AT least a year."

That was how my first boss, the king of Wall Street Larry Fink, welcomed me to the industry in the summer of 1983. Given that my initial terms of employment at First Boston only called for a two-year commitment on their part, I knew I had better get to work if I ever hoped to get a crack at the firm's mortgage trading desk. I quickly appreciated that information and relationships mean everything on Wall Street. With the support of Fink and others, I did get that trading opportunity, and stayed at the firm until 1990.

While modern technology has brought real change to Wall Street over the last three decades, the industry remains centered on the principles of competition, information, value, and relationships. Not that these principles are always brought to bear for the benefit of investors. While inside, I learned that the more I embraced these tenets, the faster I could advance and succeed. But what about everyone outside?

For most Americans, Wall Street may as well be a foreign country. This occurs both by default and by design. Regrettably, those inside the industry are not at liberty to talk openly about how the industry *really* works—and only a very few people on the outside, with meaningful industry experience, have dug deeply into Wall Street's canyons to explain how it operates, especially within the realm of regulation. That's why so many people around the world still don't understand what really happened on Wall Street in 2008 to bring our markets, economies, and nations to their knees.

With so much pain and anxiety emanating from the financial sector, questions quickly developed that to a large extent remain unanswered even today—executives, legislators, and regulatory officials are more interested in protecting their own interests than those of the public.

This was when I decided to launch my blog *Sense on Cents* (senseoncents.com), and subsequently to write this book. I believed I could help people understand much of what transpires in our economy at large and on Wall Street specifically, and I felt compelled to do it. I had no idea, back in 2009, what lay ahead.

The only agenda I had while writing this book was the pursuit of truth. Certainly the truth seems to come in a variety of shades these days. I hope my readers would agree that my desire to help people is its own most worthy goal. I try to achieve this by digging into what are often largely unread documents, full of arcane details, pertaining to issues and cases with broad impact. To do this effectively, I had to learn a lot about how other jobs on Wall Street—the ones I never had—work. Luckily, I discovered early in my professional career that if you want to get ahead, you had better know your stuff and add real value. As such, I knew that learning how the economy, markets, and securities worked from both a macro and micro standpoint was critical. And I also realized that an inquisitive mind and an appreciation of fundamental, technical, and psychological analysis of the markets would be beneficial to my readers.

I've learned a lot more fascinating stuff in this pursuit than I ever knew while working at the large Wall Street banks. I strongly maintain that the rank and file worker on Wall Street also knows little of these paths, especially within the world of financial regulation.

In fact, I believe that much of what lies along these paths is intentionally kept secret. The more I discovered, the more I wanted to learn—and none of it was good. I have special empathy for those directly impacted by the failures of our regulators. The personal stories of many whistleblowers and countless individuals involved in the Madoff, Stanford Financial, mortgage frauds, auction-rate securities, and sundry other scandals are what drove me to dig deeper into how banks could have been so irresponsible and regulators so ineffective. I am humbled by the fact that well over a million people have visited my blog and that I have had numerous opportunities to share my knowledge via major media outlets.

Let me be clear: I love Wall Street. I enjoy the pace and relish the competition of the marketplace. Our nation needs vigorous and robust capital markets if we are to promote true free market capitalism. And Wall Street itself is overwhelmingly populated with great people. I count myself fortunate to have worked with incredibly talented people and to count so many as great friends. In fact, many have encouraged and endorsed my writing. I do not believe Wall Street is a zero-sum game, nor should it be run that way. Investors, consumers, taxpayers, and their capital need to be fully and properly protected. We need to expose the corrosive if not corruptible partnership that is the revolving door between Wall Street and Washington so that the public interest is truly protected. We need financial police who are not in bed with the industry and merely writing parking tickets, but rather true watchdogs who are concerned with the public welfare. In the same fashion, we need real political representatives who are not operating with hat in hand, filling their campaign coffers under the guise of public service. Our nation is suffering under both these constructs. Without real transparency and proper safeguards, investment capital will move elsewhere—and then we all lose.

There is absolutely no way that I could have launched my blog or written this book if I were still working at any of the major Wall Street banks. Transparency and its accompanying truths are too often stifled by those in positions of power and influence. I hope this book serves to pull back the covers on Wall Street, Washington, and the regulatory agencies so American taxpayers, and investors and consumers everywhere, might see what's really going on. And I hope the exposition and discussion does not stop after these pages. If they do, the book will not meet my hopes and expectations. I hope further discussion ensues across the full spectrum of topics broached so that the truth may be further pursued, to the public's benefit.

ACKNOWLEDGMENTS

THERE ARE A NUMBER OF PEOPLE I WANT TO THANK FOR their support of my efforts. I want to thank those who will read this book and might encourage others to do the same. I am honored that you might consider my effort worthy of your time and interest. I hope my writing lives up to any level of expectation that you may hold. I want to thank those who read my blog and fuel my passion. I am humbled by and grateful for your interest and support. I am eternally grateful to my literary agent, Cynthia Zigmund, for reaching out to me and inquiring, "How come you have not yet written a book?" Her inspiration and guidance have been invaluable. This book never would have happened without her. Similarly, I want to thank Laurie Harper for her assistance and direction at the very early stages of this process. I also want to thank my editor Emily Carleton and all those at Palgrave Macmillan for having confidence in me as a first-time author. I needed a publisher who had as much faith in me as I have in myself. I am truly grateful.

I want to thank my children. The honor of being their father is the greatest gift I will ever have. Nothing is even a close second. Ultimately the messages within my writing at my blog and in this book are directed to them. I hope they will competitively pursue, and live in, the truth across all aspects of their personal and professional lives. I want to thank my folks for embracing and instilling a value system predicated on the virtues of ceaseless competition and unbridled integrity that lie at the very core of this work. I am not capable of properly thanking my beloved Valerie. None of this ever would have or could have happened without her. How I was ever so fortunate to marry her I will never know. I dedicate this book to her.

ONE
PILLOW TALK

"I agree with Madoff whistleblower Harry Markopolos' claim that FINRA is corrupt and incompetent [and] in cahoots with the large broker-dealers at the expense of the investing public."

—Joseph Sciddurlo, in an article by John Crudele
in the *New York Post*, June 27, 2011

THE YEAR 2008 WAS UNLIKE ANY OTHER WALL STREET had experienced in a long time—if ever. The demise of the once-proud underdog Bear Stearns and its fire sale to J.P. Morgan for $2 a share touched off more anxiety than most people in the markets could stomach. Yet Bear's decline was mild compared to what lay ahead.

The government takeovers of mortgage giants Freddie Mac and Fannie Mae were cataclysmic and indicative of the serious structural issues in our nation's housing market. An expedited $85 billion bailout of insurance giant AIG may have temporarily calmed the waves on Wall Street, but it only stoked the rage burning on Main Street as investors watched their retirement accounts plummet.

The failure of Lehman Brothers in September 2008 rocked the world and led to a shotgun marriage of Merrill Lynch and Bank of America. The pace of developments on Wall Street was mind numbing. The market volatility was even worse.

With barely time to catch one's breath, this tumultuous year was capped off when the largest Ponzi scheme ever perpetrated on Wall Street came crashing down. Bernie Madoff may have been the face of this particular scam but, for many people in America, "Wall Street" as a whole had become dirty words.

In the midst of this turmoil, brokers, bankers, traders, salespeople, and back office reps scrambled to keep their own heads above water. Getting business done became exceptionally difficult, if not impossible, as market liquidity dried up. The once proudly displayed badges of honor that went to top firms for providing that liquidity and best execution became objects of ridicule. Senior management on Wall Street went into full crisis mode to protect their franchises and firms' capital. International investors were aghast at the tsunami overwhelming their own markets. Add it all up, and late 2008 was about one word: survival.

The American public felt their trust had been violated and expressed their disdain at a Wall Street that seemed to run one way. The trust between investors and their banks, financial planners, and advisers was seriously ruptured if not totally broken. The rage fueled the launch of both the conservative Tea Party and liberal Occupy Wall Street movements. In the midst of these uprisings, America's collective disgust with both Wall Street and Washington intensified.

As in any relationship, before trust can be rebuilt and integrity restored, questions need to be asked, and truths revealed. Chief among these truths are the effects of the crash, more than five years after the first tremors of the economic crisis:

1. Long-term unemployment figures indicate approximately one in seven eligible workers in our nation is unemployed or underemployed. The overall rate of labor participation in America is the lowest in 35 years.

2. More than one in five children in America now lives in poverty.

3. Record numbers of our fellow citizens are now subsisting on food stamps.

Are these statistics merely indicative of an economy slow to recover from a cyclical decline? Not by any logical reasoning.

The issues strangling any sort of meaningful economic recovery in America are truly structural. To properly address them, we must expose those on Wall Street and in Washington who profited handsomely from the major cracks in our financial regulatory foundation. These cracks were built into the system long ago, and have widened—by design—over the years. And what have our central bankers, policy mavens, and political heavyweights been doing instead of addressing the cavernous holes in our financial regulatory framework? They've been propping up the same opaque financial artifice that profits financial institutions while burdening investors and consumers. Examples of the financial gamesmanship that continues on Wall Street include:

- Excessive hidden fees and expenses in investor retirement accounts
- Equity, commodity, and derivatives markets operating with little to no transparency
- Investment funds that remain littered with poorly underwritten loans
- Investors shortchanged by the manipulation of benchmark indices, including an array of overnight interest rates (e.g., Libor), currencies, and commodities
- Lack of meaningful credit availability even for creditworthy customers

- Predatory credit card rates
- A repressive monetary policy implemented by the Federal Reserve that punishes savers and fixed income investors for the benefit of banks and other financial institutions

And while all this goes on, the adjudication of even the most egregious financial fiascos remains token at best. The Securities and Exchange Commission (SEC) pursues and the US attorneys prosecute numerous individuals engaged in insider trading in little more than show trials, hoping the public will be distracted and confuse these efforts with bringing justice to Wall Street. In reality, the deep institutional crimes perpetrated on Wall Street have gone largely unpunished. The fines imposed on the firms represent nothing more than a cost of doing business—pennies on the dollar. And penalties for individual senior executives? Not in our current system of payoffs from Wall Street to Washington. Among the widespread institutional frauds that went unchecked:

- Improper foreclosure practices within the mortgage industry, including the use of a heinous practice known as "robo-signing" (i.e., rubber stamping) of documents
- Misappropriation of customer funds at commodities broker MF Global
- Money laundering at Wachovia Bank, HSBC, and Standard Chartered Bank et al.
- Widespread manipulation of the overnight interest rate known as Libor
- Improper sales practices utilized in the distribution of a wide array of structured products that would be easily recognizable as violations of the Securities Exchange Act of 1934

The token fines levied in these and other situations have revealed Wall Street's regulators as little more than meter maids.

Meanwhile, with each passing day our economy languishes, our citizens suffer, and the world's confidence in America wanes. The dichotomy between what passes for justice on Wall Street and on Main Street has given rise to a palpable disgust—laced with an unhealthy but increasingly prevalent cynicism—with the crony capitalism that permeates our nation. To stop it, we must face the truth about our structurally impaired financial regulatory system, a truth the folks on top have been desperately covering up for decades now.

What was *really* going on in our financial markets?

Where were the SEC and other financial regulators, and what were they really doing?

How could things on Wall Street have gotten so far out of control that the American taxpayer needed to step in with trillions of dollars in subsidies and bailouts?

While Wall Street itself tried to weather the storm with Washington bailouts, global investors searched in vain for safe harbors. Even after the bailout funds came through, Wall Street firms kept the hatches battened down. Investors were left to wonder what had happened to the regulatory lifeguards, and if or when real guardians of investors and the public interest might reappear.

President-elect Barack Obama stepped into this fray in January 2009 with his mantle of hope and change. Certainly, our nation as a whole and our markets specifically needed plenty of both to clean up the mess. To lead this charge, President Obama nominated career regulator Mary Schapiro to be the new head of the SEC.

Two days prior to Schapiro's scheduled confirmation hearing on January 15, 2009, the *Wall Street Journal* ran a scathing review of Schapiro and her tenure at the Financial Industry Regulatory Authority (FINRA).[1]

Who is FINRA? In its own words:

The Financial Industry Regulatory Authority (FINRA) is the largest independent regulator for all securities firms doing business in the United States. FINRA's mission is to protect America's investors by making sure the securities industry operates fairly and honestly. All told, FINRA oversees nearly 4,270 brokerage firms, about 161,765 branch offices and approximately 630,345 registered securities representatives.

FINRA has approximately 3,440 employees and operates from Washington, DC, and New York, NY, with 20 regional offices around the country.

FINRA serves every U.S. investor—from newlyweds planning to buy a home, parents saving for a child's college education to seniors depending on a secure retirement.

Every one of the 57 million American investing households FINRA serves has unique needs, but all rely on one thing: fair financial markets. That is why FINRA works every day to ensure investors receive the basic protections they deserve.

Every investor deserves fundamental protections when investing in the stock market. Whether Americans are investing in a 401(k) or other thrift, savings or employee benefit plan, or in a mutual fund, ETF or variable annuity, FINRA works every day to ensure that:

1. Anyone who sells a securities product has been officially tested, qualified and licensed.

2. Every securities product advertisement used is truthful, and not misleading.

3. Any securities product promoted or sold to an investor is suitable for that investor's needs.

4. Investors receive complete disclosure about the investment product before purchase.

FINRA touches virtually every aspect of the securities business—from registering and educating industry participants to examining securities firms; writing rules; enforcing those rules and the federal securities laws; informing and educating the investing public; providing trade reporting and other industry utilities; and administering the largest dispute resolution forum for investors and registered firms.

When rules are broken, we take action—meaning we can fine, suspend or expel firms or individual brokers from the business. We frequently require firms to return money to investors who have been harmed. In this role of "cop on the beat," FINRA ensures that all investors receive the basic protections they deserve—regardless of what kind of financial product they buy or who sells it to them.

FINRA is dedicated to investor protection and market integrity through effective and efficient regulation of the securities industry.[2]

Under Schapiro's watch at this Wall Street self-regulatory organization (SRO), fines collected and cases brought had dropped significantly. Yet, with most eyes in America focused on the abysmal track record compiled by the SEC, FINRA slipped below the radar. Schapiro was not only nominated for the top post at the SEC, but she also sailed to an easy confirmation.

As a career regulator, Schapiro appeared to be anything but the take-no-prisoners sheriff many believed was badly needed to clean up our financial industry. She seemed to be more a part of an old problem than part of a new solution. But indeed, FINRA itself was a great unknown. To those on Wall Street trading desks, FINRA are the folks you don't want to cross, for fear of having your securities licenses suspended or revoked.

Most people don't know that Wall Street as a whole is largely a self-regulated industry. While the SEC is the government's officially designated financial police, FINRA is an industry-funded, self-regulatory organization—Wall Street's own private police detail.

In what can only be defined as a coronation, the congressmen and congresswomen at Schapiro's hearing spent little time reviewing her experience at FINRA but plenty critiquing the former chairman of the SEC, Christopher Cox. Major periodicals and the mass financial media had a field day skewering the SEC for its failures not only to pursue high-profile cases, including Madoff and Stanford Financial, but also a wide array of insider trading and abusive sales practices on Wall Street. With very few exceptions, the media played right along with the Washington power base in tarring the SEC under Chris Cox while neglecting to thoroughly investigate Wall Street's self-regulator FINRA under the leadership of Mary Schapiro. While there was certainly plenty to critique about Cox's tenure, the United States learned little of substance about Schapiro and FINRA amid a healthy dose of pontificating and posturing from both the committee and the prospective chairwoman herself. Chris Cox was yesterday's news. Mary Schapiro was today's main course.

America deserved to hear Schapiro answer the hard questions about the true relationships between the SEC and FINRA and the bankers they were charged with monitoring. If the SEC under Cox was being scrutinized for its failures, clearly FINRA deserved the same scrutiny, if not more, given that it was funded by the very banks it oversaw. Despite President Obama's campaign promise of change, this confirmation hearing was an indication that things were far more likely to stay the same.

Although FINRA may talk a good game, actions speak louder than words. Largely unknown to the American public, FINRA was clearly ground zero for much of the 2008 earthquake that rocked Wall Street and roiled our nation and the world. The obvious question hanging over FINRA, given that it is funded by the industry it monitors and is charged with protecting investors, is, can a regulator serve two masters?

As a frame of reference, FINRA was formed only in 2007, as a result of a merger between the longstanding National Association of Securities Dealers (NASD) and the regulatory arm of the New York Stock Exchange (NYSE). If you dive deeply into FINRA's most recent annual reports, you will learn that this nongovernmental, not-for-profit SRO has a balance sheet ranging between $4 billion and $6 billion, and has maintained a large, diverse investment portfolio for its own benefit.

As you can imagine, this causes some very real conflicts of interest.

A multibillion-dollar balance sheet is not exactly small, especially for a regulatory organization. Where did all that money come from? Over and above that, what did FINRA hold within its own investment portfolio? While most regulatory organizations would typically place their cash in Treasury bills or an equivalent sector to avoid even the slightest appearance of a conflict of interest, FINRA has had an array of investment positions including holdings in equities, bonds, hedge funds, private equity, and even auction-rate securities (ARS).

Talk about conflicts of interest. FINRA likes to think of itself as the cops on the Wall Street beat, but this regulator was also playing in the games along with the institutions it was supposed to be overseeing.

It's not a stretch to think that Wall Street's private police might gain preferential treatment from the banks in managing their investments. FINRA's internal compliance and controls could not claim the appearance of no conflicts of interests, much less that they had no *actual* conflicts of interest.

This is the line of questioning Mary Schapiro should have faced during her hearing. Regrettably, Senators Chris Dodd (D-CT) and Chuck Schumer (D-NY) and other committee members (both Democrats and Republicans) never touched these sensitive topics. The committee clearly wasn't interested in a contentious interrogation. And so investors lost out, again. Well, I thought if our elected representatives aren't going to demand transparency, we'll have to open the doors to this private police organization ourselves.

My review of FINRA's annual report revealed a wealth of details about its investment portfolio, but none more astonishing than FINRA's holding of approximately $650 million of ARS.[3]

For those of you unfamiliar with the massive ARS debacle, allow me to give you a quick overview. On February 14, 2008, the ARS market had totally frozen. These once highly liquid securities, which had been marketed and distributed as the equivalent of cash, were really little more than another Wall Street-engineered Ponzi scheme. The success of the regular auctions at which existing ARS holders could liquidate their positions was predicated upon new buyers entering the market. Unbeknownst to most investors, many ARS auctions had been manipulated by Wall Street banks for a number of years to give the appearance of a healthy market. In February 2008, reacting to the stress and strain running across all market segments, the banks totally backed away from the $330 billion ARS sector. The ARS auctions failed, and investors' cash was frozen. Many individual investors, both large and small, had been encouraged to park their retirement funds in ARS and were now unable to access their cash. Panic ensued, and anxiety still persists for many thousands of these investors. The Madoff scam pales in comparison to the size and scope of the ARS debacle.

Where was FINRA in all of this? FINRA had its own significant investment in ARS. And without knowing for sure how FINRA handled its ARS investment, we do know categorically that FINRA did not formally post on its website that the ARS market had frozen until a few months after the fact.

Instinctively, experienced traders and investors could easily project how an institution, privy to sensitive information, might cash out before the window closed.

Every other ARS investor in America deserved to know how FINRA managed its ARS holdings. And *every* American deserved to know whether Wall Street's SRO was subject to the same rules and regulations as all other investors.

America learned nothing of substance about FINRA from the Schapiro confirmation hearing. In fact, my guess is that most investors didn't even pay attention. And the fact that she was presented as the right person for the job, despite plenty of information within FINRA's annual report and the *Wall Street Journal* article to warrant rigorous questioning of her tenure, should have been a red flag for investors and a nation trying to recover from this historic financial fiasco.

A few weeks after the Schapiro charade, Harry Markopolos, the whistleblower who exposed Madoff's operation to the SEC, raised additional red flags in his congressional testimony. Unlike Schapiro, Markopolos pulled no punches in describing the SEC as Keystone Cops and lambasting FINRA as being in bed with the industry.[4]

Did Markopolos mean that FINRA was literally corrupt or merely conflicted? All you need to do to find out is follow the money and embrace the fact that information is everything.

The collapse of our markets and our economy was a function of our large Wall Street banks and many of their international competitors being strangled by self-inflicted, nonperforming loans and securities. The enormous losses attached to these positions would have collapsed the system if basic rules of accounting had been applied. Rather than face this stark reality, Congress compelled the Federal Accounting Standards Board to change its rules after Washington had provided the widely contested $800 billion bailout to Wall Street. This capital may have saved our Wall Street banks, but it came at the expense of basic principles of capitalism. The concept of "too big to fail" became an unquestioned truth on Wall Street and across our economy. We would learn soon enough that "too big to fail" seemingly connotes "too big to trust," as well.

Meaningful transparency and financial regulatory reform are the keys to rebuilding trust in our financial markets. President Obama promised as much in his campaign; America looked for him to deliver. One could only surmise that a significant measure of that reform would have centered on FINRA.

Senator Chris Dodd (D-CT) and Representative Barney Frank (D-MA) were charged with leading the effort to bring reform to our financial system. As respective leaders of the Senate Banking and House Financial Services committees, Dodd and Frank were the logical choices to head this effort, yet both had long fed lavishly from the very financial trough they would now try to reform. In the end, politics carried the day and their leadership was never seriously questioned.

From consumer banking to investment banking, from cash products to derivatives, from customer business to proprietary trading, there were as many angles and opinions on reform as there were constituencies. In the midst of this rewriting of financial rules and regulations, it was no surprise that powerful Wall Street lobbyists were out in force. This lobby had worked tirelessly to advance the cause of their Wall Street clientele over the past few decades; they were not about to cede this turf without a fight.

Dodd, Frank, and their respective committees debated throughout 2009 on how to reform the financial system. Meanwhile, our chief central banker, Ben Bernanke, and Secretary of the Treasury Timothy Geithner exhausted capital—real and political—to save the system. Having bailed out Wall Street, Bernanke, Geithner, and other political operatives in Washington sought to regain favor by generating as quick and large a return on their "investment" as possible.

But the return on bailout funds depended on allowing these very same banks the upper hand in their pursuit of revenue and profits. Not surprisingly, expediting the maximization of revenues for a select number of financial institutions is not necessarily consistent with the rebuilding of a sound regulatory foundation.

Real financial reform requires real financial reformers, who understand the key areas of structural weakness in the system and will fight fiercely to address them. We needed political leaders and statesmen, with no agenda other than our national well-being, to execute this critical mission. If tackled correctly, these public servants would find and appoint regulators who would properly rebuild our regulatory foundation. Regrettably, from the top down in Washington, we got nothing of the sort.

In response to the reform legislation led by Dodd and Frank, the United States Chamber of Commerce released a report entitled "U.S. Capital Markets Competitiveness: The Unfinished Agenda," in which it highlighted:

The Dodd-Frank Act left nearly every pre-crisis regulator intact and failed to address longstanding, fundamental weaknesses in the system. While increasing the workloads of the existing agencies, the Act did not introduce the critical infrastructural and process changes within agencies needed to restore regulatory efficiency and effectiveness. . . .

The problem with U.S. regulation is not its quantity, but its quality. Well-run businesses depend on well regulated markets, and no legitimate business can compete in a marketplace that is not fair and transparent. The goal should never be less or more regulation, it should be better regulation.[5]

These realities are an outgrowth of the opaque political process in Washington. The lack of transparency and subsequent accountability make a fertile nest for those who are more concerned with self-interest than national interest. And our financial regulatory system—as well as, it should go without saying, the industry that nurtures it—are no exception.

Unprotected, on the outside looking in, were global investors who had worked diligently to assess risks of all types and track the flow of funds through various market channels. Little did they know the real risk in the markets stemmed from the corrosive flow of funds from Wall Street to Washington. The veil of protection offered by financial regulators disguised a dangerous web of real risk stemming from an incestuous relationship between financial and political cronies.

TWO
THE MONEY TRAIL

*Wall Street can do math, and the math looks like this: Wall Street +
Washington = Wild Profitability. Free enterprise? Entrepreneurship? Starting a business making and selling stuff behind some
grimy little storefront? You'd have to be a fool. Better to invest in
political favors.*

—Kevin D. Williamson, *National Review* Online,

December 28, 2011

WHILE IT IS OFTEN SAID THAT THOSE WHO FORGET HIS-
tory are doomed to repeat it, do not think for a second that our current economic crisis is due to a lack of financial historians. In looking
back on the markets and global economy over the last century and
a half, there may certainly have been some slow learners among our
financial titans, but the overwhelming reason for the current fallout
is the lack of a quality regulatory system.

The crisis is a direct result of the financial elites on Wall Street
working in concert with their political partners to neutralize meaningful regulatory oversight. Before we dive into that, though, let's
take a step back and look at past crises. We will quickly see that the
more things change, the more they remain the same.

The Panic of 1873 started in Europe with excessively easy mortgage money (Sound familiar?). The bursting of the subsequent bubble in the residential real estate markets caused a credit crunch in London banks. The crisis crossed the Atlantic and brought a three-year depression upon the American economy, which was already weighed down by speculative loans made to railroads and railroad-related real estate. More than 10,000 businesses failed.

Only 20 years later, our own Panic of 1893 was also driven by speculative investments in railways. Another credit crisis ensued, causing 15,000 businesses, 600 banks, and 74 railroads to fail.

Still not appreciating that a little bit of properly administered regulation may curtail a whole lot of economic pain, America then endured the Bankers' Panic of 1907. The catalyst for this financial crisis actually occurred a year earlier. The San Francisco Earthquake of 1906 precipitated the withdrawal of gold bullion from major money centers, which led to the failure of brokerage firms and ultimately a crisis of confidence among bank depositors. Many businesses failed and the stock market experienced a 50 percent decline. Even the efforts of the United States Treasury were not sufficient to stem the economic disaster. Instead, America's most widely renowned and well-capitalized banker, John Pierpont Morgan, stepped into the fray and redirected funds among banks to stabilize the financial system.

Only after three major crises in 40 years did our political leaders consider that some form of meaningful financial regulation might help restore, and maintain, order. Despite the efforts of the business community to thwart it, Congress passed a stopgap measure, the Aldrich-Vreeland Act, in 1908 to shore up the banking system. A few short years later in 1913, Congress passed the Owens-Glass Federal Reserve Act, creating the Federal Reserve.

Yet even with the newly launched central bank, the 15-year cycle of market turmoil continued when the crash of 1929 sent us spiraling into the Great Depression. This downturn, more complex and severe than its predecessors, had a number of causes. Chief among them were global economic imbalances, European nations overwhelmed by debt and taxes, and a speculative investment boom during the Roaring Twenties. By 1933, unemployment levels were near 25 percent. At last, Wall Street's efforts to forestall financial regulation were overwhelmed by the populist reform forces behind President-elect Franklin Delano Roosevelt.

On March 29, 1933, President Roosevelt directed Congress to pass legislation that would put "the burden of telling the whole truth on the seller" of securities.[1] Wall Street still strongly preferred that investors, not the government, judge the merits of new stock offerings. But by this point their political capital was limited, and the first piece of meaningful financial regulation, the Securities Act of 1933, was passed. In truth, this first step had glaring deficiencies: it regulated only the issuance of new stock offerings and penalties for violations of the act were limited to civil measures. Given the obvious shortcomings in the Securities Act of 1933, FDR went back to Congress in early 1934 for additional measures.

Newly proposed legislation called for: 1) regulation of stock exchanges; 2) registration of all securities, not merely new issue stock offerings; and 3) prohibition of virtually any manipulation of the markets. The president of the New York Stock Exchange, Richard Whitney, railed against the reform, warning of dire consequences for our capital markets and economy. His predictions that the capital markets would "dry up" and the nation would experience "tremendous, if not universal, withdrawal" of public companies from the stock exchanges were a standard Wall Street argument, but they were completely unfounded and little more than conjecture.[2] Lobbyists were successful in forcing a rewrite of the newly proposed legislation, but they couldn't take all the teeth out. The Securities

Exchange Act of 1934 became the law of the land, finally bringing some meaningful oversight to the Street. A few years later, the new reforms caught Richard Whitney himself in their web. The once proud NYSE president was sent to Sing Sing to serve five to ten years for embezzlement. They also created our nation's top financial police force, the Securities and Exchange Commission (SEC).

Given that this legislation is still on the books today, one wonders how recent actions on Wall Street could have gone unpunished. Section 10(b) of the Securities Exchange Act of 1934 prohibits, in connection with the purchase or sale of securities, "any manipulative or deceptive device or contrivance in contravention of such rules and regulations as the commission may prescribe as necessary or appropriate in the public interest or for the protection of investors."[3] This rule served as the precursor to an even broader prohibition on fraud, SEC Rule 10(b)–5, which states:

> It shall be unlawful for any person, directly or indirectly, by the use of any means or instrumentality of interstate commerce, or of the mails or of any facility of any national securities exchange, (a) To employ any device, scheme, or artifice to defraud, (b) To make any untrue statement of a material fact or to omit to state a material fact necessary in order to make the statements made, in the light of the circumstances under which they were made, not misleading, or (c) To engage in any act, practice, or course of business which operates or would operate as a fraud or deceit upon any person, in connection with the purchase or sale of any security.[4]

While FDR was resolute in seeing that the new financial reforms were passed, his choice of Joseph P. Kennedy as the initial head of the SEC was seen by many as a backwards step in establishing meaningful regulation. The Kennedy family patriarch was not only a major fundraiser for Roosevelt, he was widely believed to be a stock manipulator himself. New rules aside, with Kennedy anointed as the nation's first top financial cop, Washington effectively said to Wall Street that it was willing to be partners more often than adversaries.

In 1938, Congress amended the Securities Exchange Act of 1934 to address transactions that took place away from the regulated exchanges in the over-the-counter markets. The amendment, known as the Maloney Act, was drafted to encourage securities dealers to organize and self-regulate their activities.[5] This undertaking, "a unique experiment in supervised self-regulation was hailed as an especially provocative exercise of governmental power by a private organization."[6] Furthermore, this initiative was to be the investment that "supplies exactly what voluntary self-regulatory attempts have heretofore lacked, power within the business itself to enforce rules and regulations requiring conduct higher in standard than even that which the government could effectively require by law."[7] As a result of the Maloney Act, the nongovernmental, self-regulatory, privately funded National Association of Securities Dealers (NASD) was formed.

Former industry insider and then financial regulator Francis A. Bonner spoke to the goals of the NASD at an industry conference in 1938:

The fundamental purpose of this effort must and should always be to make our business better and cleaner and keep it so. But if we go no further than that we have not fully realized our opportunity and there may be no doubt whether the project will endure. A feeling of righteousness alone, however important, is not enough. There must be more concrete results, yielding measurable value to membership. Unless out of this is forged a sounder, healthier, more virile over-the-counter market, enabling all of us better to provide a fundamental service to the national economy, on a lasting basis, we have failed in our full opportunity.[8]

Setting a high bar for a newly launched initiative is one thing, but subordinating the self-interests of the industry for the general welfare of investors is a lofty goal. Not surprisingly, the NASD has fallen woefully short of the standard set by Bonner and his industry brethren. In 1965, a quarter century after its inception, Boston College law professor Tamar Hed-Hofmann outlined in detail how the NASD failed to uphold its initial vision. Although it was launched as a self-regulatory entity, Hed-Hofmann highlights a perhaps more accurate underlying motivation:

Lastly, the involuntary aspect of the voluntary organization must not be overlooked. The securities industry was not given a choice between self-government and no government. It was given a choice between self-government and Governmental government. The industry chose the former. Its philosophy of self-regulation is based on the theory that if the industry does not do it, the government will; therefore, the industry had better do it. The necessity of taking the public interest into account comes in through the back door. It is the means of keeping the government out rather than the realization that serving the public is one of the goals of the industry.

The attitude towards public interest is one of the important elements for consideration in evaluating the limitations and advantages of self-regulation. We may conclude that the NASD and the Exchanges, do not, as do the professions, consider the public interest as one of their goals; rather, the NASD and the Exchanges consider it as a means to an end.[9]

Hed-Hofmann's scathing review exposed the fallacy of the NASD's charter, and FINRA (NASD's successor) faces many of the same issues to this day. It is loosely organized, more motivated by self-interest than for the benefit of the investing public, and dominated by the strongest firms: "It would seem that the main reason for the broker dealer's laxity of performance is the lack of knowledge on the part of the customer. He is the only one who has the interest and opportunity to check on the broker, but his inadequate information leads to inefficiency in the agent's performance. The Special Study of the SEC found the NASD policing of the broker's activities to be faulty."[10]

Self-regulation, on the surface, may not appear to be a problem, but the rigor needed to properly police an industry as large and powerful as Wall Street requires those heading the SRO to display an uncommon level of leadership and character. We have witnessed little of this mettle throughout the history of this organization. As Hed-Hofmann exposed, "the NASD is essentially a trade organization . . . it had proved incapable of establishing accepted standards of behavior for the activities of the trade . . . the NASD had the tools and the power to use them yet failed to do so. The reasons for this failure would seem to be the diversity of membership and the conflicts of interest . . ."[11]

Ultimately, Hed-Hofmann defined the NASD as a "private police power," and describes self-regulation as being appealing simply because "it is less expensive to the government."[12] Those outside of Wall Street and Washington, especially those who have lost their life's savings, have certainly not meaningfully benefited from the expense savings given the SRO's ineptitudes.

Thirty years after Hed-Hofmann properly defined the NASD and its shortcomings, the regulator undertook an organizational restructuring "to regain investor confidence, stave off criticism from ongoing investigations by the Justice Department and the SEC, and generally improve the association's image, which had been tainted by a recent price-fixing scandal and a reputation for regulatory permissiveness."[13] Clearly nothing had changed.

While Mary Schapiro and her colleagues at the NASD stuck to a standard script promoting the supposed benefits of the mid-90's restructuring, the evidence from the '60s, '90s, and today shows this organization confronting the same issues of lax oversight, managerial dominance by the largest firms, and a prioritization of profit for both the industry and the regulator. Contrary to its conflicted public presentation, the NASD is in reality more a bridge between Wall Street and Washington than a fortress for the protection of investors. By keeping the government largely out of the financial regulatory process, the NASD has married itself to the industry and the revenues that go along with it.

The same dynamic has evolved between our elected officials and the financial industry in general. Our congressional representatives face pressure from all corners. Even if they are wont to promote grassroots initiatives, too many of them are helplessly under the thumb of party leaders and special interests. The pursuit of money to fund their operations and campaigns compromises their ability to stand and act on principle. And this perpetual campaigning and fundraising is as much out of necessity as design. In 2009, Robert G. Kaiser hit this topic repeatedly in writing *So Damn Much Money:*

> Not addressing problems has become easy in a political environment distorted by money. Money allows politicians to run for office without even mentioning important matters that affect ordinary American's lives . . . In these three decades when money became so important in Washington, Congress lost much of its

effectiveness as a governing institution. Running for re-election became more important than running the country, or keeping an eye on the exercise of executive power—the roles the founders envisioned for the House and Senate . . . The money needed to sustain this situation can be easily raised from the interests and individuals for whom the politician can do favors of many kinds.[14]

Leon Panetta, a former member of Congress, Chief of Staff in the Clinton White House, and President Obama's CIA director, says that "legalized bribery has become part of the culture" in Washington. Members of Congress "rarely legislate; they basically follow the money . . . They're spending more and more time dialing for dollars." Panetta laments the quality of people now running for Congress, echoing the conclusion reached by former senator and current Defense Secretary Chuck Hagel (R-NE) and other old hands: "It's all about winning, it's not about governing anymore."[15]

The pursuit of money dominates the Washington political process. Seats on the Congressional finance and banking committees are the most desired for the simple reason that they provide access. With hands held out soliciting campaign contributions from Wall Street banks on one side, our elected officials are not about to take them to task with the other. In February 2009, former International Monetary Fund (IMF) chief economist Simon Johnson said as much in an interview with Bill Moyers:

BILL MOYERS: When I watched the eight CEOs testify before Congress at the House Financial Services Committee earlier this week, I had just finished reading a report that almost every member of that Committee had received contributions from those banks last year. I mean in a way that's like paying the cop on the beat not to arrest you, right?

SIMON JOHNSON: I called up one of my friends on Capitol Hill after that testimony, and that session. I said, "What happened? This was your moment. Why did they pull their punches like that?" And my friend said, "They, the Committee members, know the bankers too well."

MOYERS: Last year, the securities and investment industry made $146 million in campaign contributions. Commercial banks, another $34 million. I mean, American taxpayers don't have a flea's chance on a dog like that, do they?

JOHNSON: It['s] a massive problem, obviously.[16]

Massive indeed. Disgraced financial swindler Allen Stanford knew how to play the "legalized bribery" game in Washington. He reportedly showered millions in gifts and lobbying upon Charlie Rangel (D-NY), Greg Meeks (D-NY), Bill Nelson (D-FL), Pete Sessions (R-TX), former California governor Gray Davis (D-CA), and the Democratic Party. It is hardly a coincidence that regulators from the SEC and NASD conveniently left Stanford alone as he liberally sprinkled his largesse on both sides of the political aisle. And only after the SEC had been sufficiently embarrassed by its failure to detect Madoff's Ponzi scheme did it go after Stanford's scandalous operations. While the SEC tried to save face, countless Stanford investors lost billions. Ultimately Stanford did face justice and was convicted for his crimes, but the damage from the longstanding ineffectual regulatory oversight had been done.

Whether legal or illegal, the bribery game in Washington is hard to police. Congress passed legislation in early 2012 addressing insider trading atop Capitol Hill, but it was hardly robust. Angela Canterbury, the Director of Public Policy for the Project on Government Oversight, agreed with American Enterprise Institute scholar Norm Ornstein. As reported by the *Fiscal Times*, "Prohibiting insider trading gets at the subject of public servants using information for their own financial gain, which will lead to more people getting caught on stock trades, which I think is useful," she said. "But what's missing now is more the sunlight on the financial gain of those so-liciting information from public servants, and how that in turn lines public officials' campaign interests."[17]

The House also nixed a provision making criminal laws about public corruption more punitive, and affording federal public in-tegrity prosecutors heightened power to probe public officials. It's become more difficult to bring a case against a public official since a 2010 Supreme Court decision, *Skilling v. United States*, undid a section of the honest services fraud law that enabled prosecutors to target state and federal officials on charges that they acted in their own financial self-interest rather than for the public good.[18]

"Lawmakers honestly don't feel they have a lot to fear from the public integrity section of the Department of Justice, and that could really turn into a huge problem," said Melanie Sloan, executive di-rector of Citizens for Responsibility and Ethics in Washington. This bill was one of the few chances to change that pattern, Sloan said. "But over in the House, they're just not anxious to let prosecutors more anxiously target public corruption and give the public a win-dow into their dealings with the private sector," she said. "If you're a legislator, why do you want to make it easier for prosecutors to go after you if you're going to do something illegal?"[19]

A wide array of political officials and many more donors and beneficiaries on both sides of the political aisle have bathed in the financial cesspool that has come to define Washington. The largesse comes with a very real price tag: industry protection.

While money has dominated politics for a long time, Wall Street and Washington took the money game to an entirely new level starting in the 1990s and continuing today. The premise that social welfare programs, primarily housing, could be promoted while both government and industry participants pocket sizable fees was an egregious sham. Wall Street's money and influence brought forth historic and destructive legislation that lies central to the economic crisis continuing to envelop our nation and the rest of the world.

In early 2009, Robert Weissman and James Donahue exposed the payoffs and quid pro quo in a scathing review entitled "Sold Out: How Wall Street and Washington Betrayed America." The report directly addressed the regulatory issues on the table in Washington after the economic crisis in 2008 and pointedly targeted the Washington power base for undermining our country's public welfare.

Weissman and Donahue outlined in detail the trail of money that flowed from Wall Street to Washington, and the rewards they reaped.

- Wall Street showered Washington with $1.7 billion in campaign contributions and $3.4 billion upon lobbyists over ten years (1998–2008). That money went from the lowest members of Congress to the President of the United States.
- 55 percent of the contributions went to Republicans and 45 percent went to Democrats.
- The financial sector showered campaign contributions on politicians from both parties, invested heavily in a legion of lobbyists, paid academics and think tanks to justify their preferred policy positions, and cultivated a pliant media— especially a cheerleading business media complex.

Where were our leaders with the vision and foresight to protect the taxpayers who pay their salaries? Feeding at the Wall Street trough.

What did the money buy? Weissman and Donahue address in specific detail the payoffs that accrued to Wall Street, including:

- The repeal of the Glass-Steagall Act, which separated commercial and investment banking activities. This act came out of the Great Depression. Former Fed chair Paul Volcker supported Glass-Steagall in the late 1990s and still does today. The expected repeal of this act allowed for the merger of Citibank and Travelers Insurance even before the formal repeal. President Bill Clinton, Treasury Secretary Robert Rubin, Senator Phil Gramm (R-TX), and Fed Chair Alan Greenspan were the primary supporters of this repeal.
- The allowance of off-balance sheet accounting, which promoted increased leverage in banks.
- The executive branch rejection of financial derivative regulation. The Commodity Futures Trading Commission (CFTC), led by Brooksley Born's effort, sought to exert regulatory control over derivatives. The CFTC was squashed by Robert Rubin and Alan Greenspan. At the time, Deputy Treasury Secretary Larry Summers told Congress that the CFTC proposals would cast regulatory uncertainty over a thriving market. In addition to Rubin, Greenspan, and Summers, Senator Richard Lugar and SEC Chair Arthur Levitt also supported the Clinton administration's push to decrease regulatory oversight.
- Deregulation of over-the-counter derivatives through the Commodity Futures Modernization Act drafted by Phil Gramm.
- Massive lobbying by the financial industry that resulted in allowing for Wall Street firms to engage in voluntary regulation. This acquiescence is the grossest example of

the inmates running the asylum. In 1975, the SEC ruled that debt to net capital ratios had to be less than 12:1. This "voluntary regulation" led by Goldman Sachs CEO Henry Paulson allowed investment banks to develop their own net capital requirements. Merrill Lynch went to a 40:1 ratio. SEC chair Chris Cox acknowledged this voluntary regulation was a complete failure.

- The globalization of self-regulation. (The United Kingdom instituted its own financial self-regulatory organization, the Financial Services Authority, via the merger of its banking supervision and investment services regulation in May 1997.)

- The total failure to police the mortgage banking industry and its predatory lending practices.

- Preemption by the federal government of a number of state consumer protection laws that would have mitigated much of the predatory lending.

- No accountability of purchasers of loans. Only the original mortgage lender would be liable for the predatory and illegal features embedded in the mortgages. This immunization of the investment banks eliminated their legal exposures and facilitated the continuation of fraudulent lending practices.

- Expansion into the nonprime mortgage market by Freddie Mac and Fannie Mae. Many politicians fed from the Freddie and Fannie troughs, including Chris Dodd (D-CT) and President Barack Obama.

- The creation of institutions now deemed "too big to fail." Weissman and Donahue conclude that Wall Street banks should now be treated like highly regulated public utilities.

- Overly compliant rating agencies that further facilitated the
  crisis. These agencies were and still are seriously conflicted
  given that their revenues are generated from fees paid by
  the banks involved in underwriting new issue securities
  offerings. This relationship and source of revenue are eerily
  similar to the ties between the Wall Street banks and their
  self-regulator.[20]

Which subsets within our financial services industry broke out
their wallets? Weissman and Donahue pinpointed the hard dollars
spent to generate such fundamental transformations on Wall Street:

Commercial Banks: $154 million in campaign contributions and
$363 million on lobbyists

Accounting Firms: $68 million in campaign contributions and
$115 million on lobbyists

Insurance Companies: $218 million in campaign contributions
and $1.1 billion on lobbyists

Investment Banks: $504 million in campaign contributions and
$576 million on lobbyists.[21]

Over the last four election cycles (2006–2012), the individuals
receiving the greatest amount of lucre have been presidential candi-
dates, but those dispensing the funds are careful to spread the money
liberally across both parties.

A very large percentage of the lobbyists "spreading the wealth"
were former government officials—the ultimate revolving door.

Even after the economic crisis—or perhaps because of it—the
lobbying dollars spent by the financial industry have only increased.

FIGURE 1.   TOP RECIPIENTS (DOLLAR FIGURES IN MILLIONS)

2012	2010	2008	2006
Romney (R-MA) 59.1	Schumer (D-NY) 5.5	Obama (D-IL) 45.0	Lieberman (I-CT) 5.6
Obama (D-IL) 21.2	Kirk (R-IL) 3.2	McCain (R-AZ) 31.6	Clinton (D-NY) 5.6
Brown (R-MA) 5.1	Portman (R-OH) 3.2	Clinton (D-NY) 22.0	Santorum (R-PA) 3.3
Boehner (R-OH) 3.3	Gillibrand (D-NY) 3.1	Romney (R-MA) 14.3	Ford (D-TN) 2.9
Perry (R-TX) 3.2	Fiorina (R-CA) 3.0	Giuliani (R-NY) 14.1	Kyl (R-AZ) 2.5
Gillibrand (D-NY) 3.0	Reid (D-NV) 2.6	Dodd (D-CT) 6.3	Corker (R-TN) 2.2
Corker (R-TN) 2.7	Bennet (D-CO) 2.4	Coleman (R-MN) 3.2	Talent (R-MO) 2.1
Hatch (R-UT) 2.1	Toomey (R-PA) 2.2	Richardson (D-NM) 3.2	DeWine (R-OH) 2.0
Cantor (R-VA) 2.1	Rubio (R-FL) 2.2	Warner (D-VA) 2.8	Nelson (D-FL) 1.9
Menendez (D-NJ) 2.0	Blunt (R-MO) 2.1	McConnell (R-KY) 2.8	Menendez (D-NJ) 1.9

Credit: Author created with data culled from "Finance/Insurance/Real: Top Recipients," Opensecrets.org, http://www.opensecrets.org/industries/recips.php?ind=F&cycle=2012 &recipdetail=A&mem=Y&sortorder=U (accessed August 28, 2013).

Over the course of the 2010 and 2012 election cycles, the flow of funds from Wall Street to Washington for lobbying and campaign contributions ran upward of $3 billion.

With so much money traveling from Wall Street to Washington, the question of how financial regulators, especially the industry-funded FINRA, began protecting Wall Street rather than investors and citizens becomes clear.

Although never openly discussed by Wall Street and Washington insiders, the simple reality is *the* source of funding for FINRA and a *primary* source of campaign contributions for Washington elites came from the same well—Wall Street. The item purchased by those funds was a compliant and lax regulatory system. The funds may have bought Wall Street the desired ineffectual oversight, but they also bought America and the world a crisis of epic proportions.

THREE
COPS ON THE TAKE

FINRA's numerous failures should hardly come as a surprise given the incestuous relationship between SROs and the financial services industry.

—Danielle Brian, executive director of Project on
Government Oversight, February 23, 2010

THE S&P 500 INDEX DECLINED 11.7 PERCENT IN THE FIRST quarter of 2009, after a 39 percent nosedive in 2008, ensuring the continued erosion of investor retirement accounts and consumer confidence. Many investors, not wanting to acknowledge the pain of these losses, had simply ceased looking at their statements. As a sanity-saving method this was understandable, but it inhibited the public from immediately inquiring and ultimately unearthing just what had transpired on Wall Street.

At this point, the departing George W. Bush administration and the incoming Obama team were clearly more focused on saving Wall Street than determining just who and what had crippled our economy. No surprise, since the evidence would ultimately implicate every administration since the Carter regime in the 1970s. Instead, Congress passed legislation providing $800 billion in bailout funds via the Troubled Asset Relief Program (TARP). These funds and assorted other financial backstops may have supported Wall Street, but would they also provide a convenient cover for the financial artifice that lay buried among the rubble?

All eyes now turned toward new SEC chair Mary Schapiro for a renewed sense of urgency in cleaning up Wall Street. Of course, she was also tasked with rebuilding and reenergizing the demonstrably ineffective SEC itself—no easy feat. During her confirmation hearing, Schapiro unapologetically laid out the significant shortcomings within her prospective new ranks, but her failure to provide meaningful review of her tenure at FINRA left those watching closely feeling very uneasy.

During her time at FINRA, Schapiro addressed the self-regulator's mandate in asserting:

> As investors navigate the marketplace of the future, there are four primary protections that must come with every financial product, from securities to insurance to mortgages. For both the peace of mind of investors and the soundness of the retail markets, investors should be able to enter into any transaction knowing that every person selling a financial product is tested, qualified and licensed; that the product's advertising is not misleading; that every product sold is suitable for them; and that there is full, comprehensive disclosure for all products being sold. As simple as this approach sounds, regrettably, not all financial products come with all of these basic safeguards. That needs to change.[1]

Was Schapiro in a position to bring about the necessary changes during her tenure at FINRA and subsequently the SEC? What had transpired at FINRA and on Wall Street that had prompted Schapiro to make this statement in the first place?

Once I began my post-crash research, I was captivated by my initial look into FINRA's financials. Time to find and follow the money. To do that, I'd need to take a deeper dive into this organization.

To my amazement, I discovered at this point in time that FINRA had an approximately $6 billion balance sheet. What was a self-regulatory organization mandated with protecting investors doing with such a large balance sheet? Managing an operation of this size was certainly no small undertaking. Digging into FINRA's financials unearthed the following:

FINRA manages a diverse investment portfolio consisting of: (i) global government (state and local) securities; (ii) corporate and asset-backed securities; (iii) equity securities; (iv) exchange-traded funds; (v) mutual and commingled funds; (vi) hedge funds; (vii) private investments; and (viii) other financial instruments or structures.

FINRA controls the buying and selling decisions of its direct investments.

. . . Also included in trading securities as of December 31, 2006, are auction rate securities with a cost and fair market value of $646.9 million.[2]

FINRA had committees and guidelines in place to mitigate the potential for conflicts of interest in the process of managing its diverse investment portfolio. Having seen similar types of Chinese walls—ethical barriers between different divisions of an institution to avoid conflicts of interest—in existence on Wall Street, I also knew that they were often more for appearance than functionality. Evidence and experience have taught us that when push comes to shove on Wall Street, financial gain and opportunity almost always carry the day. Not surprisingly, when questioned about specific situations regarding FINRA's investment activities, committee members were evasive.

How could an entity such as FINRA think that investors and other interested parties would not be baffled to learn that Wall Street's own private police were playing in the games that they were charged with overseeing? In other words, the cops in the financial casinos were not only manning the eye in the sky and walking the floor, but they also had a seat at many of the tables and their own chips in the games. This reality was certainly not common knowledge to those working on Wall Street or to investors.

Can FINRA uphold its mandate to protect investors while simultaneously managing its own investment portfolio and its relationships with the Wall Street banks and brokers that provide its funding? At the very least, most market participants would have assumed that given FINRA's regulatory position in the marketplace, they would not have any control whatsoever over the buying and selling of the assets in its portfolio. After all, how would market participants ever know if FINRA gained access to inside information and then acted upon it, as opposed to upholding its mandate to protect investors? Talk about a high-wire act without a net. What we didn't yet know was that we were the ones really walking the tightrope, not FINRA.

FINRA does have a board of directors, an office of the ombudsman, and is also officially monitored by the Securities and Exchange Commission. The burdens placed upon these overseers are substantial. In the immediate aftermath of the 2008 crisis, the question of conflict within FINRA reverberated throughout the country; in the ensuing years, with no answer provided, the ringing has only become shriller.

In what hedge funds was FINRA invested? With which dealers did FINRA execute most of its business? Whatever happened to

FINRA's holdings of those hundreds of millions of auction-rate securities (ARS)? Prior to addressing these disclosures or lack thereof further, let's revisit FINRA's mandate, "that there is full, comprehensive disclosure for all products being sold."

If in fact this segment of FINRA's mandate was upheld to the very letter of the law, Wall Street would be a very different place. Regrettably, the concept of full, comprehensive disclosure is all too often just window dressing, buried in the legalese of financial documents and fund prospectuses. If investors actually did take the time to properly review a prospectus prior to investing, they would be challenged by the fine print, the disclaimers, and even the fact that prospectuses are usually not delivered until after the transaction has been completed.

Investors are typically left at the mercy of their financial planners and brokers to interpret the finer points of a wide array of investment offerings. Even if you can find the disclosures embedded in a prospectus, being able to properly interpret and understand them is something else entirely, especially for retail investors.

Plus, most investment offerings and financial products are intentionally vague in terms of detailing the true embedded risks. Disguising risk is an art form on Wall Street. Bankers are exceptionally creative in structuring products that seem attractive to investors while simultaneously driving revenue for their firms. Someone with institutional expertise might be able to spot where the risks lay, but retail investors—and often even retail brokers—are hard pressed to do the same.

The regulators like FINRA and the SEC are supposed to step into this muddy area and protect investors. In the midst of an engagement with FINRA representatives, I promoted an idea that has had many proponents but no traction with regulators: a simplified Outline of Risk Parameters, available upon request, written in plain

English, aimed primarily at retail investors but also institutional investors, if so desired.

I envisioned it as a supplement to the official prospectus for each investment offering. The parameters could provide a simple description and numerical grade for degree of risk for each of the following components:

1. Market Risk
2. Interest Rate Risk
3. Liquidity Risk
4. Volatility Risk
5. Credit Risk
6. Prepayment Risk
7. Currency Risk
8. Structure Risk
9. Counterparty Credit Risk
10. Extension Risk
11. Transparency Risk

In addition to these risk parameters, a prospectus and offering memorandum should highlight in bold print—and in one spot—*all* of the fees, charges, loads, expenses, and other costs associated with the product or transaction, delineated in layman's terms.

If these parameters had been in place prior to the market meltdown, regulators would have been in a much better position to protect investors and dealers alike. Such an outline would not have precluded the possibility of financial fraud on Wall Street, but it certainly would have highlighted risks and mitigated losses.

Let's explore what risk management tools and techniques the self-regulator FINRA might have utilized in the process of managing its own portfolio. Did it receive special consideration from the

Wall Street community in terms of sharing risk management strategies? This sharing of proprietary practices would not be all that uncommon for Wall Street's most favored clients, including the largest hedge funds and most active traders. But even more importantly, did FINRA gain access to proprietary information—material, non-public information—that it could utilize in the management of its own investment portfolio? While the sharing of risk management tools is simply an accommodation for a priority client, the sharing of proprietary information begins to tread over the line into illegal behaviors.

Who polices the police? Who regulates the regulators? During periods of calm and equanimity in the markets, these questions might be considered moot. But during periods of crisis, they couldn't be more germane.

Numerous hedge funds imploded during the market crisis. Did FINRA have exposure to any of these? Numerous structured transactions cratered in value. Might FINRA have taken a hit on any of these? A variety of private investment vehicles disallowed investors from cashing out their holdings. Is it possible that FINRA could have been negatively impacted in its daily management and oversight of Wall Street as a result of any or all of the above? With so little transparency in FINRA's portfolio, we may never know.

There was plenty of smoke around many market segments leading into the crisis, but just a handful of enormous fires enveloped a large percentage of investors in 2008. The highest-profile was the scam perpetrated by Bernie Madoff. But even larger was the $330 billion market for a supposed short-term, cash-surrogate instrument, known as ARS.

Could it be possible that Wall Street's self-regulator FINRA had any funds exposed to Madoff? What a bombshell that would be. Bernie and family members had longstanding relationships with many professionals inside the industry and at FINRA's predecessor, the NASD.

Whether on the Madoff front or so many others, the pain and anguish experienced by consumers, investors, and taxpayers beginning in 2008 and still ongoing today have been very real. The anxieties running throughout the United States and many other regions of the world might only be mitigated by getting to the truth and enacting appropriate remedies and real justice. Those procedures would be totally dependent on one factor: transparency. This virtue always sells well on the stump for politicians and regulators promising to clean up Wall Street.

President Obama evinced the spirit and virtue of transparency on the day of his inauguration by stating, "Those of us who manage the public's dollars will be held to account—to spend wisely, reform bad habits, and do our business in the light of day—because only then can we restore the vital trust between a people and their government."[3]

Shortly thereafter, in a memo written for the heads of executive departments and agencies, our new president put forth a very populist message:

> My Administration is committed to creating an unprecedented level of openness in Government. We will work together to ensure the public trust and establish a system of transparency, public participation, and collaboration. Openness will strengthen our democracy and promote efficiency and effectiveness in Government.
>
> Government should be transparent.
>
> Transparency promotes accountability and provides information for citizens about what their Government is doing.[4]

Presumably, the new head of the SEC, Mary Schapiro, read the memo promoting greater transparency and disclosure in tending to the people's business. In fact, in the process of providing her own testimony to the Financial Crisis Inquiry Commission, the supposedly nonpartisan entity launched by the Obama administration to learn what really caused the economic crisis, Schapiro referenced the need for greater disclosure and transparency upward of 40 times.

While these principles always sound exemplary and reasonable in speeches and in testimony, in practice they often run headlong into the brick wall of individuals and firms who would suffer professionally and financially as a result. At these critical junctures, only those with real character can determine whether disclosure and transparency will carry the day.

Can you imagine what our recent history and our foreseeable future would be if borrowers and lenders alike were required to provide and support verifiable data in the mortgage origination and underwriting process? This was the job of the regulators in the years leading up to the crisis—and they dropped the ball in a spectacular fashion. This failure has made for excellent political theater over the last several years. Our nation has had to suffer through endless debates between the far wings of our respective political parties as to whether we need more or less regulation. Regrettably, the debate itself has been badly misdirected. Instead of debating whether our nation needs more or less regulation, we should have been aggressively debating and exposing the real cracks in our regulatory foundation. These not so small fissures encompass the very nature of the regulatory model, including special emphasis on the self-regulatory organizations overseeing much of our financial markets; the financials and specific details of how our regulators were actually managed; and the *real* truth behind the failures of the regulatory organizations along with their conflicts of interest.

We did get a bit of congressional bantering among politicians looking to score political points, but little of any real substance came out as a result. Although that's no real surprise, America had the right to hope for real change this time, given the magnitude of the financial losses and government bailouts from the taxpayers' money.

Without knowledge of the specific holdings in FINRA's portfolio, no one could ascertain if and how conflicts of interest played out within the organization. Naturally, efforts by individuals as well as a broker-dealer, Amerivet Securities, to attain that information were rebuffed by the organization.

"We disclose a great deal of public information in our annual reports, far more than we are required to do," says Herb Perone, a spokesman for FINRA. "Our records are not open for public examination."[5]

So much for greater transparency and disclosure. We will likely never learn if FINRA's asset-backed securities consisted of subprime mortgage holdings. We will also likely never know the real nature of FINRA's investments in hedge funds, exchange-traded funds, or any other holdings—or indeed, whether FINRA ever compromised itself and its regulatory responsibilities for its own financial benefit.

Except that, perhaps unintentionally, the folks at FINRA had actually left an amazing clue in the report detailing their investment portfolio. Instead of writing that FINRA held a generic position in a money market–like fund or a short-term bond fund or a cashlike equivalent, FINRA's only specifically detailed investment holding was laid out as "auction rate securities with a cost and fair market value of $646.9 million."[6] The scent from this lead was phenomenal.

Luckily for investors, in early 2009 a new kind of whistleblower came upon the scene and displayed the actual practice that so many politicians and regulators merely preached. Harry Markopolos made a huge splash upon Washington as he exposed massive holes within our regulatory agencies and their specific failure to protect investors from the swindler Bernie Madoff.[7] This financial sleuth doggedly tracked Madoff for the better part of a decade, and exposed the SEC as a sideshow, citing the following specifics:

1. The SEC was totally incompetent and neglectful through-out the entire Madoff affair. He provided the SEC with reams of evidence and tips for them to pursue. They never fully investigated.
2. There were significant turf battles between the SEC offices in Boston, New York, and Washington, DC.
3. Markopolos claimed it took him a mere five minutes in reviewing Madoff's reported returns to know they were suspect. It took him approximately four hours to confirm his suspicions by reviewing options trading volumes.
4. He recommended one governmental financial regulator to oversee all of the other regulators so that all information is shared and tips are fully and properly pursued.
5. He provided 29 separate red flags on the Madoff fraud.
6. The largest feeder fund to Madoff was Fairfield Greenwich.
7. There are 12 other funds in Europe that have provided a significant flow of capital into Madoff. Markopolos planned on releasing those names to the SEC.
8. Madoff attracted a lot of dirty money, including funds from the Russian mob and Latin American drug cartels.

Markopolos maintained that Madoff must have had a "lot" of help in perpetrating this fraud both inside and outside of his office. And despite the fact that there were times when he feared for his life, Markopolos offered to go undercover for the SEC to fully reveal Madoff's scam.

In regard to the SEC, Markopolos maintained that the commission did not have the degree of professional expertise to detect, investigate, and pursue cases. Subsequently, he recommended that the SEC should hire seasoned financial professionals and pay them on an "incentive basis" to unearth and process financial frauds. Despite receiving no compensation for a decade's worth of work, he was obsessed with his pursuit in order to rid the system of a criminal fraud.

In regard to investors, America's new champion recommended that, going forward, every money manager and investment adviser *must* have separate custodians to handle investor funds.[8]

The media picked up on Markopolos's story and made him a household name and a nationwide hero overnight. While Markopolos received extensive acclaim for his dogged determination, it could only be properly viewed in the context of the disdain for the incompetence displayed by the SEC.

The size, scope, and tawdriness of the Madoff scam captured the nation's imagination. There is no doubt that the pain created by this villain was very real. Yet, Madoff actually provided the industry a very convenient scapegoat. With all the focus on an amoral individual, Wall Street as a whole was afforded significant cover at a time when real public pressure and investigative work into a wide array of financial frauds should have been ongoing. To this end, Markopolos actually provided another strong lead by highlighting that, in his opinion, while the SEC was simply incompetent, the NASD and its offspring FINRA were "in bed with the industry."[9] Markopolos pointedly referenced that the regulators at FINRA missed a number of failed and fraudulent practices, including the ARS market.

Did FINRA miss these frauds due to incompetence, or intentionally? The ARS market was a $336 billion market in which virtually every Wall Street dealer was involved. If ever there was a market segment deserving of real attention it was this. Investors ran the gamut from large institutions to small retail clients. With the release of FINRA's report, we learned that the very regulatory body charged with protecting investors in this market had its own chips on the table too.

How did this all play for investors in ARS? As reported in April 2009 by *Bloomberg*:

> Investors who were sold the securities as money-market alterna-tives say Finra, a non-profit corporation owned by banks that oversees 5,000 brokerage firms and 659,000 brokers, failed to protect them. The market froze in February 2008 when banks, which had supported the debt for two decades through periodic dealer-run auctions, stopped buying bonds that investors didn't want as losses from subprime mortgages spread. 'Nobody was de-fending any investors,' said Mike Offit, a 52-year-old real estate capital markets consultant in New York.[10]

What had FINRA done with its own ARS? Had it held them throughout the market meltdown and the eventual total freezing of this multi-hundred billion dollar market segment? Or did it cash out from the ARS table, sell its bonds, and save itself millions of dol-lars while leaving tens of thousands of other investors stranded with hundreds of billions of dollars in ARSs?

Is FINRA operating as an effective self-regulatory police force, or just as crooked cops on the take?

FOUR
OUT IN THE COLD

The Financial Industry Regulatory Authority, supervising 344 investor arbitration cases over auction-rate bonds, skirted losses from the securities by selling its holdings months before the market collapsed.

—Darrell Preston, *Bloomberg*, April 29, 2009

WALL STREET IS EXCEPTIONALLY TALENTED AT STRUC-turing esoteric investments and then figuring out how and why investors should be interested in purchasing them. This process is a core part of functioning capital markets. The flow of funds from those willing to take the risk of investment to those willing to take the risk of borrowing to fund and grow an enterprise is central to our economy. Without the flow of capital, there is no capitalism.

The wide array of investment products traded on Wall Street runs from the very simple to the exceptionally complex. Typically, investments with longer maturities and durations are riskier. The risks can take the form of simple market risk, heightened inflation, credit downgrade, or structural breakdown within the investment itself. Shorter term securities, while certainly not risk-free, typically have mitigated risks. Treasury bills, short-term certificates of deposits, money market funds, and bankers' acceptances are seen almost as cash equivalents, and thus have historically attracted a lot of interest and capital from institutional and retail investors alike looking for a safe place to park their cash. Although the crisis of 2008 affected every market sector, these cash-equivalent sectors fared the best in terms of liquidity.

Given the depth of this liquidity, Wall Street structured a vehicle to feed the seemingly insatiable demand for cash alternative investments while simultaneously providing financing for a wide array of borrowers. Welcome to the world of auction-rate securities (ARS).

Given the fact that ARS were promoted as cash-equivalent investments, one might logically assume that the entities borrowing the funds from investors had short-term cash needs. But no. The entities tapping the ARS market for financing typically had very long time horizons on those borrowings. For example, one ARS financing brought to market on behalf of Jefferson County, Alabama, in 2002 had a stated maturity of February 1, 2042. Yes, a stated 40-year maturity on a security marketed and sold as a cash-surrogate. Only on Wall Street could you get away with that kind of equivalence.

The borrowers included entities like colleges and universities, hospitals, utilities, student loan companies, and corporations. A large percentage of ARS were issued by municipal entities.

This method of borrowing funds was so attractive that large asset management companies entered the market and started using it within investment offerings utilizing a fixed amount of capital, more commonly described as closed-end mutual funds. These securities were designated as auction-rate preferred securities.

What made them so attractive to borrowers? Their ability to access long-term funding at interest rates benchmarked to the short-term market. If that sounds too good to be true, it's because it is. Yet this market segment had functioned since the mid-1980s and peaked at $336 billion. It could not possibly be a scam. Or could it? For perspective, $336 billion is the approximate equivalent of 2 percent of our nation's annual GDP.

Suffice it to say, the ARS market was not small, and virtually every Wall Street firm was involved. From large firms like Merrill Lynch and J.P. Morgan to smaller, downstream shops such as Oppenheimer & Company and E*Trade, ARS traded very actively and were generally perceived as safe, liquid, and as good as cash.

As the name attests, the valuations and market for ARS were set at auctions, which typically occurred every 7, 14, 28, or 35 days depending on the specific security. Naturally, the fact that the underlying borrowings often had maturities of 30 to 40 years was generally not highlighted in the sales process. This lack of disclosure, seemingly harmless during periods of calm in the market, would soon pose larger problems for the market as a whole.

The interest rate on individual ARS resets as bids came into the market from new buyers. Once a sufficient number of buyers came into the market, the highest interest rate necessary to clear the market—that is, to sell all of the available ARS—would be assigned to it until the next auction. Certain ARS issues were structured with technicalities that made them exceptionally difficult to explain to the average investor. These nuances were lost on many investors, and many brokers as well, who were getting increasing pressure from their management to get rid of growing ARS inventories, even years before the crisis. Again, during periods of market calm the auction process appeared to be smooth and fully functional. As with many things on Wall Street, however, appearances were deceiving.

Of course, there's a name for a market operation predicated on new cash being raised from new buyers or entrants in order for existing investors to sell their holdings. Its progenitor was an individual in Boston in the early 1920s who was trading stamps. Charles Ponzi became notorious for his singularly run enterprise, and since then countless other scam artists, including Bernie Madoff, have played the same con. While the ARS market is not a prototypical Ponzi scheme, it looked and operated in very similar fashion.

With auctions occurring so regularly, salespeople all over Wall Street treated ARS as just another investment offering in the basket of cash-equivalent securities. The hook they used to bring new clients into the mix was the fact that ARS yielded just a slightly higher rate of interest than a typical money market fund. What customers didn't see were the decidedly higher sales commissions and payouts to salespeople for moving this product.

Before long, a lot of cash and ARS were changing hands, and Wall Street was making a tidy profit. In the middle of this ARS casino stood FINRA, equal parts traffic cop and market participant.

Any market, but especially one the size of ARS, needs regulations enforced and regulators held accountable in order to protect investors. What were the specific issues that confronted regulators and investors in this market? In May 2006 the SEC brought a case against virtually all of the big firms on Wall Street—including Goldman, Sachs & Co., J.P. Morgan Securities, Inc., Morgan Stanley & Co. Inc., Bear, Stearns & Co., Citigroup, Lehman Brothers, and many others—alleging that between January 1, 2003 and June 30, 2004 "without adequate disclosure, certain Respondents bid to prevent auctions from failing. . . . Without adequate disclosure, certain Respondents submitted bids or asked investors to change their bids so that auctions cleared at rates that these Respondents considered to be appropriate 'market' rates."[1] Collectively these charges can be defined as market manipulation.

This case demonstrates how long the corruption in the market had been going on. If the Wall Street dealers were compelled to effectively manipulate ARS auctions so as to give the appearance of a healthy market in this supposed cash-equivalent security, had there ever been solid ground beneath them?

In FINRA's predecessor the National Association of Securities Dealers' (NASD) annual report for 2004 they classified their ARS investment as "either preferred stock or bonds with interest rates that reset periodically, typically less than every 90 days, based on a Dutch auction process. Given the longer-term maturities of these securities, they are classified as available-for-sale investments, rather than cash and cash equivalents."[2]

FINRA knew that the securities themselves were not cash equivalents, even though they were marketed as such by Wall Street. And, given the SEC action against the vast majority of Wall Street firms in 2006, FINRA must have also known that beginning at least as far back as 2003, ARS auctions were being manipulated by Wall Street banks to give the appearance of a healthy market. Yet the SEC and FINRA took no meaningful actions against the banks for manipulating the auctions. In typical fashion, the banks were allowed to effectively walk away without admitting or denying the findings, and with a token $13 million fine for the headache. A slap on the wrist of that sort for an industry that generates tens of billions of dollars in quarterly revenues is little more than a cost of doing business and not about to change behaviors within a market segment as large and profitable as ARS.

We got resounding proof that nothing had changed when the ARS market totally failed in early 2008. Despite the SEC action, and perhaps because the penalty had been so light, Wall Street banks had continued to manipulate the ARS market. But when the crisis hit, it went the way all Ponzi schemes eventually must: Sellers wanted out and new buyers did not show up. In mid-February 2008, this once supposed "cash-equivalent" market froze, and along with it the cash holdings of countless investors and billions of dollars.

Panic ensued among investors when they learned that they could not gain access to "their" cash. Investors were understandably irate, and brokers had little to offer in terms of solace, or even meaningful information. Many brokers were being stonewalled by their own management.

Later, these same investors learned from complaints—often brought by state regulators—that senior management at a number of institutions had actually dumped their own personal holdings of ARS as the market showed signs of stress. Information about market distress and insiders selling their securities was conveniently withheld from investors. And what was FINRA doing during this period of 2007 and early 2008? Recall that FINRA was not only the regulator charged with protecting investors, but that it also managed its own investment portfolio, including a not insignificant $650 million in ARS.

The ARS market represented approximately 10 percent of the total US money market and a similar percentage of the municipal bond market. The size of this market and the scope of the investors that utilized the ARS market were so extensive that it's almost hard to fathom. The ripple effect of a hiccup, let alone a total freezing of the ARS market, would be substantial throughout our nation's economy. What did FINRA do?

In late April 2009, *Bloomberg* exposed FINRA's fecklessness. *Bloomberg* reported, "The Financial Industry Regulatory Authority, supervising 344 investor arbitration cases over auction-rate bonds, skirted losses from the securities by selling its holdings months before the market collapsed."[3]

According to Ed Dowling, an ARS investor who is a clothing manufacturer in New York City, "If they had these securities, they had to know the market was in trouble."[4] FINRA provided no meaningful evidence to refute Dowling's assertion or those of other

ARS holders, most of whom were reluctant to speak out in public for fear they would jeopardize their chances of getting their cash returned. During that very critical juncture in 2007, FINRA chose not to protect Dowling or other individuals as was its mandate, and instead chose to protect itself by liquidating its own ARS position and keeping quiet about the status of the ARS market. Dowling made a public plea that I posted on my blog:

Is there some legal authority out there who is willing to investigate what could turn out to be the biggest scandal in this whole auction rate securities mess? I realize you guys are tired of hearing from me, I'm tired of writing you. Unfortunately for both of us this is still a necessity for me. You're lucky, you can just delete this. I have to keep writing if I ever expect to see my money again.

You see I know I've been robbed. Maybe some of you are not sure if this is really a robbery? Maybe you are so busy ARS are not high on your priority list? Maybe ARS victims that haven't figured that out yet that they have been robbed deserve to lose their money, I don't know. I don't fall into that category.

I fall into the category of people who fell for the illusion of investor protection. The banks owning FINRA, who owned ARS, who sold all their ARS, at just the right time, and never mentioned it to the rest of us, who owned ARS, sold to us by the owners of FINRA, who neither admit or deny any wrong doing, after they were forced to return what they stole and pay large fines, is a little too much for me to come to terms with.

Also seeing Mary Schapiro's signature on the FINRA 2007 financials which show their ARS holdings, then having you guys tell me if I wanted to file an official complaint about FINRA I had to do so with the SEC, then having Obama appoint Mary

Schapiro to the head of the SEC who I'm going to have to complain to, egh—the illusion of protection.

To think I filed an official complaint with FINRA and have spent countless hours over the last year e-mailing and calling them hoping to get a little justice, what a farce. Oppenheimer & Co used my trust to rob me and that's bad. A FINRA betrayal, that's much worse.

Is the SEC, AGs, politicians, etc., going to investigate FINRA in earnest or help them cover this up? Will FINRA be required to divulge (with proof) all their activity with ARS? Shouldn't all questions about their involvement in ARS be answered before the ARS class action suits begin?

You would think that somebody out there might want to know why FINRA decided not to mention their dealings in auction rate securities. Is there anyone interested in why the FINRA investment advisory board decided to advise FINRA to move almost a billion dollars in cash out of ARS right before the market was collapsed, by their owners?

Are we going to end up in arbitration against the companies that sold ARS to FINRA and possibly advised FINRA to sell their ARS because the market was going to collapse?

Is the government serious when they say they want to restore investor confidence or do they just want to recreate the illusion they are protecting us so we believe we can be confident to invest again?

Ed Dowling[5]

In a feeble attempt to deflect investor outrage, but in a manner that would not pass muster with Dowling or anybody possessing a degree of common sense, FINRA spokesman Herb Perone told *Bloomberg,* "FINRA didn't know the auctions were poised to

weaken."[6] Not until late March 2008 did FINRA issue its first guidance for ARS investors entangled in this massive mess.

If we were to believe Perone, we would have to accept that
FINRA was totally unaware of the SEC action in 2006, as well as
the pronouncements made by the NASD in its own annual reports
from 2003 to 2005 acknowledging the fact that ARS were not cash
equivalents. We would also have to conveniently overlook statements
made by Mary Schapiro, who stated in October 2008, "Yet, while
many individual investors were lured into buying auction rate securities last year, institutional investors and companies were dumping
their shares. . . . In 2006, institutional investors owned about 80
percent of all auction rate securities. But by the end of 2007, that
number had plummeted to 30 percent."[7] A transfer of approximately
$165 billion in ARS from institutional—and regulatory—hands to
Mom and Pop, who don't know any better.

With regulators like this, why bother having protection at all?
From FINRA's perspective, it was to convey a sense of calm when
investors should have been feeling cautious. "It was for cash that
we needed to have parked for a temporary period of time," Perone
said. "It was common to take cash you needed to hold and put it in
auction-rate securities."[8]

Perone once again conveniently forgets to mention that FINRA's
predecessor, the NASD, did not account for its ARS holdings as
cash given the long-dated maturities of the underlying borrowings.

With the knowledge of FINRA's self-protecting liquidation of
ARS mere months prior to the failure of the entire market, FINRA's
subsequent warning regarding developments within the ARS market can only be defined as pouring salt in an open wound.

In early April 2008, FINRA posted the following: "In response
to current market conditions, some issuers are offering partial redemptions of auction rate securities. This *Notice* reminds firms that

when allocating partial redemptions of auction rate securities among their customers, they must adopt procedures that are reasonably designed to treat customers fairly and impartially, and must put their customers' interests ahead of their own."[9]

Talk about shameless. After FINRA showed itself to be totally ineffectual in protecting investors, it offered direction to the Wall Street banks as to how they should dispense the medicine it was unwilling to swallow itself.

In mid-2008, the Federal Reserve and other officials throughout Washington were well aware that our banking system was ready to implode. They were also well aware that the $336 billion of ARS had been improperly represented as cash-equivalent investments. Rather than step in and mandate that the banks and brokers involved in the willful and intentional misrepresentation of these securities (clear violations of the Securities Act of 1933 and the Securities and Exchange Act of 1934) repay their clients, the Fed intervened with the SEC and slowed the process of making investors whole, that is, being repaid in full. While violating the property rights of investors and effectively aiding and abetting a fraud, the Fed determined that our banking system needed the capital invested in ARS more than the endless stream of investors who had paid it in the first place. Unbeknownst to investors, they were now not only battling their banks and brokers for the return of their cash, but the regulators and the Federal Reserve as well. Little wonder it took so long for ARS investors to receive attention, let alone be recompensed for their losses. And the media, so quick to cover the Madoff scandal, widely ignored this much larger and more damaging fraud.

Five years after the fact, thousands of ARS investors are still short billions of dollars. While selected investors have been made whole, often in a random fashion, others continue to hold out for the return of their money.

Aside from the continuing risks borne by investors, the human suffering from the ARS mess is almost indescribable. Countless individuals and families were unable to manage their lives and businesses without being able to access their money. Businesses closed down. Children could not go back to college. Retirements were put off. And little to no justice was dealt to those who had clearly violated securities laws.

Years after the market had initially frozen, institutions including BlackRock, Pimco, and Oppenheimer still hadn't fully reimbursed their ARS investors. Their defenses were full of glib remarks like, "There is no guarantee that all or a portion of a particular fund's ARS will be redeemed"; "No explicit word on when or whether their investments will be redeemed"; and "It isn't possible to determine if and when a solution will be identified."[10]

The words spoken by the following ARS investors are far more powerful than the empty platitudes put forth by the likes of Herb Perone and other regulators or the empty promises emanating from Washington or Wall Street. These words reflect the pain and anguish of our fellow citizens. Hundreds of commentators at my blog shared their disgust and frustration at not being able to access their money while FINRA, now replete with its own hundreds of millions of dollars from its liquidated ARS, provided little meaningful assistance.

Marsha, April 20, 2011

I too have been burned by the ARS mess. I own Jefferson County, Al. water & sewer ARS sold by Morgan Keegan. I moved my account to Raymond James when the @#$# hit the fan. I have had good service in other areas at RJ but I am repeatedly advised to hold tight, that I will be made whole when the water/sewer board is able to refinance the debt. Mine was a 35 day commitment and the broker lied to me, and without permission, put all of my ARS cash in the same Jefferson County instrument. My business is struggling because of this mess. Does anyone else own Jefferson County ARS and do you have any advice as to what to do now?[11]

Kathy, April 20, 2011

Seemingly according to Alvarez and the Federal Reserve the banks needed the cash more than the individuals and institutions to whom it belonged. After three years of fury at having been defrauded, I am more furious than ever. I was one of the people who filed a complaint with the SEC. I followed it up. I called them, and got "investigators" to return my calls. They seemed so sincere. They were patsies at best. I have wondered for three years how a $330 BILLION fraud so central to the collapse of our economy could go virtually undiscussed. I wondered why Congress held a hearing, and then essentially talked about something else. I have my answer, after three years. The fix was in. They had the money, and they decided to keep it, because they could. Now someone tell me what I'm supposed to believe in when I hear "United States Of America." I have lost my trust.[12]

JoanZ, April 16, 2011

Been reading you and following your concern for all of us who own ARS. It's been three years and my husband is 81 and I can't wait for ARS to be redeemed any longer. I started arbitration against the financial advisor who sold them to me and I am finding it will be a very expensive as I have to get a lawyer since he has one. The ARS he sold us are BlackRock and MFS two very active financially rich companies. My question is who is responsible to get my money returned? . . . The financial adviser who advised us to purchase them ??? and why can't BlackRock and MFS give back our funds after three years? I have since left the adviser as of course I lost faith in him. It seems I have no choice but to go to arbitration but of course I could lose and it will cost a lot of money as well. What to do??? Thanks for being there and keeping this terrible injustice alive.[13]

Susie, July 21, 2010

Raymond James sold me Nuveen muni ARS instead of treasuries (which I suggested) and has stonewalled for 2 1/2 years. My broker keeps telling me Nuveen will redeem them. What do you think? Are regulators going after RJ? My kids' college money is locked up—legal fees will eat up too much of it, secondary market is a huge hit.[14]

Wink, July 1, 2010

I'll add to the above the rude, hostile treatment I've received at the hands of Oppenheimer. They're just mean, bitter people who have no regard for clients. For the uninformed, the Massachusetts complaint vs. Oppenheimer asserted that senior management sold their own private ARS holdings upon hearing that the auction rate market was tanking, and neglected to notify their clients. Is this who you want managing your money? AVOID OPPENHEIMER LIKE THE PLAGUE.[15]

Dave, November 16, 2011

What Oppenheimer did to its clients is worse than anything Jerry Sandusky did to those boys. And no, comparing opco to alleged pedophiles is not a stretch. Same with N.Y. regulators. Scum, scum, scum, scum. My elderly mother is without food or medicine thanks to Oppenheimer and nobody gives a damn.[16]

Dave, November 16, 2011

I contacted over 20 lawyers who specialize in going after bro-kerages and because I *only* had several hundred grand frozen nobody would handle my case. Not worth their time. One even laughed when I tried to explain about my mother, saying, "Not pertinent, dude. The arbitration panel doesn't give a #$%^ about Mama."[17]

So much for liberty and justice for all. I brought this story re-garding FINRA's ownership and liquidation of ARS to the atten-tion of the SEC's inspector general, who redirected me to the SEC's Office of Compliance Inspections and Examinations (OCIE). I provided all of what I had unearthed from FINRA's and NASD's reports, as well as the details of FINRA's ARS liquidations. I was informed that the OCIE does not provide feedback on information provided to it. Sadly, I was not surprised that I never heard or saw anything else about it.

FIVE
KANGAROO COURT

It just isn't right that the only way the millions of people who work at banks or do business with them can resolve their disputes is through a kangaroo arbitration system overseen by Wall Street itself.

—William D. Cohan, *Bloomberg*, January 12, 2012

ONE MIGHT EXPECT THAT THE DAMAGE FROM THE auction-rate securities fiasco would be expeditiously addressed by those overseeing the settlement of disputes within the financial industry. After all, the ARS investors had not knowingly purchased a highly complex structured product. They had not searched for incremental yield by navigating down the credit curve or into speculative investment vehicles. They merely believed what their brokers told them—that is, that ARS were a cash-equivalent security. So any dispute over this simple security should have been a slam dunk on behalf of the investors. But I'll bet you can guess how it turned out.

Individuals investing in the markets or working in the financial industry know, on some level, that our markets are filled with risk. Regrettably, far too few, especially at the entry level, appreciate the very real risks of dispute resolution on Wall Street. Level playing fields? Fair and equitable treatment? Reasonable people providing rational assessments and deliberate findings? Perhaps at the outset prospective customers and employees are assured of these things, but once money and precedent are on the line, all bets are off.

When opening an account or joining a Wall Street firm, customers and employees are required to sign an agreement that all disputes will be adjudicated via an arbitration process. But who wants to think about dispute resolution and arbitration when entering into a relationship? With no choice in dispute resolution other than arbitration, individuals opening an account with a broker or financial planner typically think little of what might go wrong, and more as to how they will allocate their assets and what sort of returns might be generated. By the same token, individuals launching a career on Wall Street focus on how they can move up the learning curve and advance into bigger and better opportunities.

Relationships on Wall Street may be stimulating and productive, but they are also fraught with risk. The anguish of failed relationships and subsequent disputes on Wall Street can be very trying and expensive. As Justice Harry Blackmun wrote in 1987 in his dissenting opinion in *Shearson/American Express v. McMahon,* a case addressing the fairness of the mandatory arbitration system in the financial industry: "There remains the danger that, at worst, compelling an investor to arbitrate securities claims puts him in a forum controlled by the securities industry. This result directly contradicts the goal of both securities Acts to free the investor from the control of the market professional. The Uniform Code provides some safeguards but despite them, and indeed because of the background of the arbitrators, the investor has the impression, frequently justified, that his claims are being judged by a forum composed of individuals sympathetic to the securities industry and not drawn from the public."[1]

Anybody pursuing justice on Wall Street typically presumes that the facts will bear out his case and the truth will prevail. If only it were so. Unlike a divorce proceeding, in which the mediator typically has no preexisting relationship with either party, when entering into arbitration against a Wall Street firm, plaintiffs should be aware of potential hurdles. Unbeknownst to many investors, the Wall Street counterparty whom you are pursuing has very deep pockets, little interest in losing money, and even less interest in allowing precedents to be set. Additionally, the regulatory body officiating the bulk of the arbitration hearings on Wall Street is funded by Wall Street—yes, the very same firms sitting across the table from you. Beyond that, the arbitrators hearing your complaint and passing judgment on the dispute are paid by the very same regulatory body charged with officiating the hearing. Yes, the same one funded by the firms you are challenging. And, as if that were not enough, the arbitrators hearing the complaint are often industry insiders—that is, they actually work at Wall Street firms. Yes, those same Wall Street firms that pay the regulatory body officiating the hearing so that the regulatory body can pay the arbitrators

Quite the spider's web, no? Suddenly, your open-and-shut case becomes a long, drawn out, torturous affair in which you face mounting legal bills in the possibly hopeless pursuit of a fair judgment.

Do you begin to see how daunting it is to bring a complaint against a Wall Street firm? This is not to say all complaints have equal merit. There are certainly plenty of plaintiffs who are willing to file frivolous complaints on Wall Street, just like everywhere else. But since the market meltdown, the arbitration process has seen a dramatic influx of very legitimate actions from very angry investors.

In 2009 there were 40 percent more arbitration cases filed than in 2008, the most since the tech bubble burst in the early 2000s. Over the last 16 years there have been approximately 6,000 arbitration cases filed per year. The greatest number of cases (8,945) was recorded in 2003, after the meltdown of the NASDAQ; the fewest cases (3,238) occurred in 2007.

The types of arbitration filings ran the gamut, but the bulk were categorized as follows for 2008–2012 (total number reflected in parentheses; note that cases could be counted in more than one category): Margin Calls (423); Churning (1,269); Unauthorized Trading (1,724); Failure to Supervise (9,756); Negligence (11,895); Omission of Facts (8,553); Breach of Contract (10,121); Breach of Fiduciary Duty (15,009); Unsuitability (8,601); Misrepresentation (11,885).[2]

What truly underlies many of the complaints brought on behalf of investors? The simple fact that Wall Street brokers are held to a suitability standard that does not mandate them to look out for the best interests of their customers.

Wall Street firms, not surprisingly, are focused on revenue. Although they may profess to put customer interests first, that principle runs a distant second to profitability. Suitability does not require that a broker looks out for his customer's best interests, but merely that he sells a product deemed "appropriate" for that client. All too often, the definition of appropriate is left unspecified. When faced with the possibility of a highly profitable trade versus selling an appropriate product, many brokers on Wall Street will not think twice about relegating "appropriate" to the back seat. In the process, the broker may very well engage in any number of the aforementioned practices, including misrepresentations, unsuitability, omission of facts, negligence, or churning—engaging in excessive trading in a discretionary account for the primary purpose of generating commissions. In fact, many of these transgressions were common practice in the sales of supposedly simple products such as auction-rate securities.

If all it took to rectify wrongs on Wall Street was laying out clearly defined facts and relying on fair-minded arbitrators to do the right thing, the volume of arbitration cases filed annually would be far greater than 6,000. For an industry the size of Wall Street, it's barely noticeable. Why so low? The hurdles are so high.

Wall Street lawyers impose a form of financial torture on investors that would make our enemies proud. Plaintiffs must provide tax returns, investment portfolios, account statements, banking information, etc., while the Wall Street firms typically delay, and delay some more. All the while, your costs are going up and your patience is wearing down.

What are these high-priced Wall Street lawyers usually trying to prove? That the plaintiff possesses a greater degree of sophistication than he actually does. And as such, in spite of any and all sales tactics—including misrepresentation—employed by the broker, the "sophisticated" investor should have been aware of the real risks embedded in specific investment offerings.

When firms on Wall Street were pushing a wide array of collateralized debt obligations (CDOs) out the door, high net worth clients were viewed as prime targets for these offerings. Of course, the mere fact that an individual is wealthy does not necessarily mean that he will fully understand the risks of a highly complex product. As Michael Slomak, a Cleveland man ravaged by a Merrill Lynch-issued CDO, declared, "We were just lambs being led to the slaughter."[3] The Slomak family lost all but $16,500 of an initial $2.65 million investment in that transaction. A standard sales commission for that deal would have paid the broker $15,000 to $20,000, or possibly much more than that. As we've discussed, many brokers don't even fully understand the highly structured and deeply risky products they're selling. What they do understand are high payouts and pressures from management to drive revenue.

When brokers and banks are not held properly accountable for even the blatant misrepresentation of supposedly cash-equivalent products, investors should not assume that meaningful protection would be forthcoming in other, more complex products.

More than half our population, approximately 160 million people, owns stock or a stock fund. More than 5 million people, or slightly less than 2 percent of our population, would be deemed an accredited investor, that is, a high-net-worth investor. By either of these measures, the level of arbitration cases filed annually, approximately 6,000 (a mere four-thousandths of 1 percent of those who own stocks), is hardly statistically significant in terms of the overall number of investors. How many investors take their lumps without even knowing it or having the wherewithal to pursue a remedy?

Be mindful that even of the insignificant number of cases filed, investors only win about half the time, and are generally awarded only half the funds requested. That is, investors making claims for $10,000 are doing well to win one out of every two times and to get paid $5,000 to settle each case. These figures amount to a return on average of 25 percent of total dollars contested. Additionally, those most likely to succeed in arbitration are those with claims against smaller broker-dealers for smaller amounts. These figures lend real credence to the maxim, "the house always wins."

As William Galvin, secretary of the commonwealth and chief securities regulator for Massachusetts, opined in 2005 during congressional testimony on the arbitration process, "The term 'arbitration' as it is used in these proceedings is a misnomer. Most often, this process is not about two evenly matched parties to a dispute seeking the middle ground and a resolution to their conflict from knowledge, independence and unbiased fact finders, rather what we have in America today is an industry sponsored damage containment and control program masquerading as a juridical proceeding."[4]

Let's look at the arbitrators themselves. Many are past or present employees of Wall Street firms, as discussed. Others are lawyers with varying degrees of understanding of the markets and investments. Just like many legal proceedings are won or lost based upon the selection of the jurors, many an arbitration case is largely predetermined by the selection of the arbitrators. Historically, the industry has controlled the selection process. "The control over the selection of arbitrators who are on the panel, and the ability to classify them as 'public' or 'non-public,' as well as other broad authority invested in the Director of Arbitration of the NASD, gives the NASD vast authority to influence the outcome of investor disputes submitted to it."[5]

After the market meltdown of 2008 and the flood of investor complaints, FINRA did file a rule proposal that would allow for plaintiffs to select a panel of arbitrators without industry representation. As FINRA's CEO and chairman Richard Ketchum weighed in, "Giving each individual investor the option of an all-public panel will enhance confidence in and increase the perception of fairness in the FINRA arbitration process. All investors will have greater freedom in choosing arbitration panels, and any investor will have the power to have his or her case heard by a panel with no industry participants."[6]

Clearly, Ketchum realized that after 2008, plaintiffs were losing confidence in Wall Street and in its arbitration process.

This proposal to allow all-public panels was fully implemented shortly thereafter, and within the course of the first year investors chose to go the route of nonindustry-related arbitrators more than three-quarters of the time. Did this portend better days ahead for Wall Street arbitration? Not so fast.

Remember, he who controls the purse strings ultimately controls the process. Arbitrators, whether public or nonpublic, are paid by the regulators that are funded by the industry. Thus, the arbitrators are effectively paid by the industry. A common refrain among lawyers and others who have participated in arbitration hearings on Wall Street is that in order to get along, the arbitrators had better go along. One law firm that has represented more than 1,000 customers in FINRA arbitrations described the problem as one in which the parties "are allowed to strike arbitrators they do not like . . . public FINRA securities arbitrators who decide too often for the customer, or award attorney's fees or punitive damages, will quickly learn that they will be struck by the brokerage firms during the arbitrator selection process or not be chosen to sit on arbitration panels."[7]

Could FINRA or the industry be so brazen as to exact revenge on arbitrators who award a plaintiff with a large settlement? In one case that raised eyebrows in the industry, three arbitrators found themselves blackballed after having awarded a plaintiff a significant settlement in a complaint brought against Merrill Lynch. Hard-hitting industry insider turned critic Bill Cohan shed some light on this case:

> After awarding the estate of the customer more than $520,000—a large amount by arbitration standards—Finra heard from unhappy Merrill executives and fired the arbitrators, two of whom had many years of experience.
>
> "You mete out justice, and then you get slapped in the face," one of the fired arbitrators, Fred Pinckney, told me in an interview. . . . "It's unbelievable that they would take such an experienced panel and get rid of it," Pinckney said. "To me, this undermines the credibility of the entire Finra process—I didn't say kangaroo court—but when you have three well-credentialed people, doing their job, and there were no meritorious grounds for an appeal, and we get handed the 'black spot'—and not all at once—it makes for a pretty cheap novel."[8]

Pretty cheap novel, perhaps, but this is the real world and a system of fairness and integrity is predicated upon people in positions of power doing the right things. Was FINRA firing three veteran arbitrators after awarding a large settlement to a plaintiff a mere coincidence? Then how does one explain the fact that FINRA reversed its decision after Cohan exposed this sordid situation? A mere three weeks after Cohan's initial expose, he reported that the arbitrators had been reinstated: "Finra's treatment of Gormly, Kolber and Pinckney—despite their reinstatements—illustrates just how shoddy the system is. It needs to be scrapped, and those with a grievance against Wall Street should get their day in a real court."[9]

A real court with real justice would be a novel concept on Wall Street, but not likely when the FINRA kangaroo-style court is ready and willing to take on all comers. Luckily, Cohan's power of the pen and the resulting public shame heaped upon FINRA did have some meaningful impact in the reinstatement of the arbitrators. But not all plaintiffs are lucky enough to have the spotlight. The lack of meaningful justice meted out is highly correlated with a resulting lack of trust in the markets and the industry overall. As further evidence of this lack of real trust in the Wall Street arbitration system, let's review the case of Mark Mensack.

Mensack served our nation for 22 years in the US Army and Army Reserves. He taught at West Point during his tenure in the service. He is one of less than 600 individuals in our nation with the designation of Accredited Investor Fiduciary Analyst. He focuses his efforts on working with all fiduciaries but especially retirement plan sponsors. Having developed a real expertise in this space, he eventually landed at Morgan Stanley to grow his business.

In late 2010, Mensack brought a whistleblower action against Morgan Stanley for what he believed was a pay-to-play scheme within its retirement accounts practice. Mensack chose to leave the firm rather than work within the business. In the process, he ran the risk of forfeiting a signing bonus that Morgan Stanley had provided him. The case ultimately ended up in arbitration, and Mensack lost despite his strongly held assertions that Morgan Stanley representatives had perjured themselves. Over and above that, Mensack claimed that the arbitrators did not have the technical understanding of the principles being broached and violated their obligation not to discuss the case.

In the annals of Wall Street arbitration, Mensack's case would likely be just another line item of an unhappy employee realizing the difficulty of taking on a Wall Street behemoth. Except Mensack's case was not yet over. Having lost the arbitration but still strongly believing in his case, Mensack filed an appeal requesting a copy of the approximately 18 hours worth of testimony. FINRA sent Mensack a recording with approximately ten hours worth of testimony. The initial copy of the testimony was clearly incomplete, so Mensack repeated his request to the case administrator while also informing the FINRA ombudsman of the problem.

In the process of repeating his request, Mensack highlighted that the testimony provided him was not missing the first eight hours or last eight hours or a consecutive eight-hour recording of testimony. No, the DVD was missing eight hours of testimony with the breaks occurring at 14 separate points in time. Those breaks often came in the middle of critically important testimony provided by Morgan Stanley representatives. Some of the breaks were literally in midsentence. Mensack proclaimed that the most significant missing portion included the entire cross-examination of a Morgan Stanley witness during which Mensack's attorney was introducing proof that the firm had fabricated evidence against the plaintiff.[10]

FINRA is obligated by its own rules to provide a recording of case testimony.

FINRA Rule 12606. Record of Proceedings

   (a) Tape, Digital, or Other Recording

   (1) Except as provided in paragraph (b) [i.e., a stenographic recording], the Director will make a tape, digital, or other recording of every hearing. The Director will provide a copy of the recording to any party upon request for a nominal fee.[11]

If this were a real court of law, Mensack would clearly have been able to make the case that his rights were egregiously violated. That said, when he continued to press FINRA on the point, ultimately he received zero satisfaction. A FINRA regional director penned the following pathetic response:

I apologize that portions of testimony are missing from the recordings for the June hearing sessions, and for any perceived miscommunications from the FINRA staff about the status of the recordings. FINRA is required to make a tape, digital, or other recording of every hearing. . . .

Unfortunately, portions of testimony returned to us by the panel are missing from the recordings for the June hearing sessions. . . . We spoke with the Chairperson E. William Pastor, who informed us that he operated the digital recorder during the hearings. Mr. Pastor stated that he believed that all testimony was recorded, and he was unable to explain why testimony is missing from the recordings. We listened to the recordings several times, and we tested the particular digital recorder used during the arbitration. We found the recorder to be working properly, and we have not been able to determine what caused portions of the testimony to be missing. We are taking steps to provide further guidance to our arbitrators on operating the digital recorders in order to prevent this situation from occurring again. . . .

I understand Mr. Mensack's disappointment with the arbitrators' decision. However, FINRA has no authority to reverse the award.[12]

The director's response rings hollow given that the missing portions occurred at 14 strategic points. We are supposed to believe that Wall Street arbitration represents a de facto, fair, and equitable judicial proceeding. More like a kangaroo court.

Pleading one's case to a group of arbitrators is hard enough, but when a plaintiff has to combat a regulatory body that is in bed with the industry—just as Justice Blackmun had opined in the *McMahon* case—then the deck is truly stacked against anyone who might look for justice on Wall Street.

SIX
INCEST

The Alliance for Economic Stability ("AES") today released publicly a letter to the Financial Crisis Inquiry Commission ("FCIC"), a body set up by the U.S. Congress to investigate the causes of the financial crisis, urging an investigation of FINRA, a self-regulatory organization. The letter states that the AES hopes the FCIC will thoroughly investigate the responsibilities and failures of FINRA in allowing the practices that were the most direct cause of the financial crisis.

—Alliance for Economic Stability, April 12, 2010

WHEN PEOPLE THINK OF WALL STREET, THEY PICTURE THE ringing of the bell at the New York Stock Exchange, the chaotic trading floors at Goldman Sachs, and the skyline of lower Manhattan. But these images belie the depth and breadth of Wall Street's actual reach.

"Wall Street" currently consists of about 4,200 firms scattered throughout every state in the union. For regulatory purposes, the broker-dealers making up Wall Street are delineated as large, medium, and small firms. The large shops have 500 or more registered representatives within their ranks. Medium-size broker-dealers have between 151 and 499 representatives. The small firms have 150 and fewer representatives. All of these firms are under FINRA's jurisdiction. And, of course, all of these firms would like to increase their revenues and grow their clientele. But that doesn't mean their interests are fully aligned.

The crisis of 2008 put extraordinary pressure on firms of all sizes. The failure of Lehman Brothers and the takeover of Bear Stearns saw the disappearance of names that had adorned the Wall Street marquee for more than a hundred years. Truth be told, though, Wall Street has been under pressure from investors since the turn of the century. The meltdown of the technology-heavy NASDAQ market reached its nadir in 2002, unleashing the heavy hand of New York Attorney General Eliot Spitzer, who exposed how ten of the largest Wall Street firms had tied their research and banking units to the procurement of new-issue-underwriting mandates and the outsized revenues that went along with them. How did investors burned by these scams respond? Many exited the markets altogether. As investors fled, the overall number of firms on Wall Street declined by approximately 10 percent. By 2007 there were just over 5,000.

Yet the closing of firms during this period hardly registered with the major players on Wall Street. In fact, after the tragedy of 9/11 and the meltdown of the NASDAQ, the easy-money policies of Alan Greenspan and lax regulation of excessive leverage allowed the five largest investment banks (Goldman Sachs, Merrill Lynch, Morgan Stanley, Lehman Brothers, and Bear Stearns) to completely dominate their smaller and midsize brethren. These five institutions held upward of 60 percent of the total assets, and garnered close to 60 percent of the total revenues, in the US securities industry.[1]

After the crisis of 2008, the demise of firms in the financial services industry accelerated due to outright failure or forced takeovers of these institutions. Of course, if not for the intervention and bailout provided by Washington, all of the major Wall Street firms as we know them would have ceased to exist. And while those bailout dollars may have saved the major firms, they did little to nothing for the small and midsize shops that were "too small to care about." Post-2008, the number of broker-dealers shutting their doors increased by another 15 percent. Wall Street may have technically survived the crash, but it was a very different place. What was missing? The cornerstone of all relationships: a real sense of trust.

Investors once again responded by pulling their funds out of the market. The declining trading volumes across market sectors further escalated the pressure on the remaining firms' bottom lines. In turn, they responded by laying off employees and exiting business lines entirely. The lack of trust encompassing the industry not only influenced the relationships between investors and their brokers and financial planners, but between investors and regulators as well. Because in the midst of the major financial scandals that dominated the headlines, one crucial fact got lost: that FINRA directed the bulk of its oversight toward the smaller and medium-size broker-dealers.

A longtime securities attorney, Mark Astarita of Beam & Astarita, a New York law firm that represents some 30 broker-dealers, echoed the sentiments of many in the industry when in early 2012 he remarked in *Financial Advisor:* "The SEC, Finra and the states have been more aggressive with smaller B-Ds, which don't have as much money for in-house counsel. 'Have you ever seen Finra fine or sanction a senior executive at a large firm?' he asks. 'They just don't do it. When was the last time they fined a senior executive at Merrill Lynch? But they will jump on the opportunity and insist that an individual at a smaller firm take a fine or suspension, personally, where at a larger firm it would be at the firm level. Individuals can't afford to fight Finra.'"[2]

Similarly, in 2012 David Shields, vice-chairman of Wellington Shields and Company and a current member of FINRA's small firms advisory board, had much the same to say when pursuing that position. Shields weighed in with his strongly held opinion highlighted on FINRA's own website: "Large firms print phone books for compliance manuals and can afford a battery of compliance officers and lawyers to fend off overzealous regulators. Small firms should not have written supervisory procedures for things they do not do. Minor offenses should not be treated as felonies. Of course the public must be served, but regulatory overkill with commensurate costs and little if any demonstrated benefit depletes the resources of honest endeavor to public disadvantage. Overregulation layers in costs that must ultimately be passed through to the customer. It is time to modify a rules based environment and move toward principles based governance."[3]

Fighting the industry-funded police is not something most people on Wall Street have the fortitude to do. But while Astarita and Shields spoke out on behalf of smaller broker-dealers, one individual went a step further. In a true David and Goliath story, a small minority-owned broker-dealer from Moreno Valley, California took legal action against FINRA.

The man behind Amerivet Securities is not like most people on Wall Street, and battling a regulator was nothing next to the other battles he has seen in the course of his career. Amerivet was owned and operated by Lieutenant Colonel Elton Johnson, a decorated veteran of the United States Marine Corps Reserve and a Green Beret who served tours of duty in Iraq and Afghanistan.

The Amerivet complaint lodged against FINRA was not the first time these combatants had engaged each other. FINRA's predecessor, the NASD, censured and fined Johnson in 1997 for violations of minimum-capital requirements and for failing to file municipal securities offerings on a timely basis. Later, FINRA suspended him as a supervisor from December 2006 to June 2008 for allegedly not properly managing an employee. Johnson maintained that the latter action was nothing more than retaliation for the fact that the lieutenant colonel brought his complaints about FINRA to none other than President George W. Bush.

These back and forth skirmishes were just the prelude to the volleys launched by Johnson in his major complaint. In August 2009, in the Superior Court of the District of Columbia, Amerivet submitted a complaint against FINRA that included the following charges and allegations:

> ... FINRA has failed in what it represents in its advertising to be its core function i.e., the protection of investors. ...
>
> From 2005—if not earlier—through 2008, FINRA failed to regulate and oversee the operations of certain large firms that are at the heart of the financial meltdown that has plagued this country. Among FINRA's noteworthy regulatory failures were Bear Stearns & Co. ("Bear Stearns"), Lehman Brothers, Inc. ("Lehman"), Merrill Lynch and Co., Inc. ("Merrill"), Bernard L. Madoff Investment Securities, Inc. ("Madoff"), Ross Mandell's Sky Capital Holdings, LLC (and related entities) ("Sky Capital") and Stanford Financial Group ("Stanford").
>
> In each of these cases and others, FINRA ignored the egregious practices and operations of these influential member firms, despite having access to the inner workings of these firms. Many of these firms are and have been under SEC and state investigations for criminal wrongdoing or have already pled guilty to securities fraud.
>
> FINRA did nothing to stop the egregious wrongdoings of these and other miscreants nor to inform the investing public that improper and illegal conduct (including massive securities frauds) was occurring on a grand scale, particularly at the six firms referred to above.

FINRA knew or should have known about the fraud being perpetrated by several of its most influential members, but there is nothing in the public record to indicate that FINRA conducted *any* oversight of these now-failed malefactors or their senior executives.

At the same time the enormous frauds referred to above were being perpetrated, many of these firms' representatives enjoyed positions of trust and authority within FINRA, including powerful directorships. These positions of influence and trust presented obvious conflicts rife with opportunity for personal and corporate financial gain at the expense of the securities markets and investors they were obligated to protect. Yet, FINRA evidently did nothing.

In its 2008 Annual report, FINRA Chairman and CEO Richard G. Ketchum acknowledged that "policymakers, regulators, and investors recognized that the U.S. regulatory infrastructure was plagued with gaps and in need of modernization." He went on to say that: "Throughout the financial crisis, FINRA has worked closely with other regulators, particularly the Securities and Exchange Commission and the Federal Reserve, to examine firm activities for compliance with FINRA rules and federal securities laws, investigate wrongdoing and, when rules were broken, enforcing those rules." There is nothing in the public record to support these statements, nor anything that begins to resemble any strenuous examinations, investigations or enforcement addressed to Bear Stearns, Lehman, Merrill, Madoff, Sky Capital, Stanford or their senior officers prior to the collapse of these firms.

Only after these firms and others precipitated a global financial crisis, and in order to promote itself and attempt to overcome the supervisory failures of its senior executives, FINRA proclaimed falsely that: "The instability in the markets, and at a number of financial institutions, heightened investor fears" and that "FINRA helped allay those fears, and foster confidence, by working to ensure the protection of customer assets at troubled institutions." In fact, FINRA had done virtually nothing to protect the public from investing in Bear Stearns, Lehman, Merrill, Madoff, Sky Capital or Stanford, despite the fact that it knew or should have known that each was precarious financially and/or operating under fraudulent pretenses.

Mr. Ketchum further stated that FINRA: "committed considerable resources to educating investors and arming them with information they needed to make sound decisions in the difficult environment . . ." In fact, whether or not such resources were "committed" generally by FINRA, they were not committed in any way to educating the investing public of the illegal and improper conduct that was causing many billions of dollars of harm to investors within FINRA's sphere of protection. Indeed, Mr. Ketchum admitted that: "Vigorous enforcement of rules and regulations is a cornerstone of FINRA's work to protect investors." In fact, with respect to the six firms identified above and others, FINRA specifically made no effort to enforce applicable rules and regulations.

Despite having done nothing of substance to protect investors prior to 2008 when its involvement and public warnings would have been helpful, Mr. Ketchum bragged that: "In 2008, FINRA focused its efforts in several areas of investor harm— including . . . auction-rate securities (ARS) recommendations and sales." As of today, according to one source, $165 billion in ARS remain frozen and out of reach of investors. There is no indication in the public record or on FINRA's own website that, until the collapse of the ARS market in 2008, FINRA provided any material warning or even information to the public with respect to ARS or the risks of investing therein.

FINRA knew ARS were not cash or cash-like even though they were marketed in that fashion as then-NASD owned ARS and did not formally account for them as cash given the long maturities of the underlying loans. Indeed, FINRA's executives unloaded the Company's own funds that had been previously invested in ARS, but did nothing to warn or protect the investing public.[4]

Beyond these very serious charges and allegations, the Amerivet complaint also addressed the exceptional levels of compensation accorded to FINRA senior executives. Specifically, FINRA chair and CEO Mary Schapiro saw her compensation increase by a not-insignificant 57 percent in 2007—from $1,999,731 to $3,140,826, plus the value of indirect benefits not readily determinable. Over and above that, she was awarded termination benefits valued at more than $7 million. All told, Schapiro's tenure at the not-for-profit, industry-funded regulator was a rather profitable experience for her personally. Her total assets of between $11 and $42 million placed her as one of the wealthiest members, if not *the* wealthiest, of the Obama administration.[5] Not a bad livelihood for Schapiro in a career spent largely in not-for-profit enterprises.

Johnson's complaint also brought unwanted attention to the high-risk manner in which FINRA managed its members' funds within its internal investment portfolio. The fact that a regulator charged with monitoring a wide swath of the markets also managed its own funds within these market segments should be troubling enough. FINRA maintained that its investment committee made sure that there were no conflicts of interest in the management of these assets. If that were the case, then every person with even a passing Wall Street interest would be interested in how FINRA responded to the following Amerivet allegation: "Upon information and belief (although it is impossible to verify without an examination of FINRA's books and records), FINRA also directly or indirectly placed substantial funds with Madoff prior to December 2008, and either sustained losses and/or may be subject to substantial 'clawback" claims in connection with such 'investments.' Obviously, if such 'investments' occurred, substantial conflicts of interest existed which would have rendered them improvident and inappropriate without regard to Madoff's now-underlying Ponzi scheme which, had FINRA performed its regulatory functions properly, would have been exposed and halted."[6]

Could it have been possible that the industry's own regulator had invested funds with the infamous con artist? Madoff had been integrally involved with the formation of the NASDAQ, the equity exchange founded in 1971 as a direct competitor to the powerful New York Stock Exchange (NYSE). In fact, he went on to serve as president for its board of directors. Several other members of the Madoff family were also involved in various functions at FINRA (and before that, the NASD), highlighted here as part of the Amerivet complaint: "Madoff was a member of FINRA [NASD] since 1960. During this period, particularly since the early 1980s when prosecutors have alleged the Ponzi scheme began (Mr. Madoff states that it began in the early 1990s), despite numerous 'examinations' of the firm and its affiliates and 19 customer complaints received by FINRA since 1999, no serious investigative efforts were ever undertaken of Madoff and its affiliates by FINRA."[7]

Clawback: money or earnings that are distributed and then taken back as a result of special circumstances.

Amerivet attorney Richard Greenfield supported the allegation that FINRA invested funds with Madoff when *Fox Business* host David Asman, on "America's Nightly Scoreboard," asked him, "How did you get information suggesting that indeed FINRA was investing with Madoff?" Greenfield responded that not only was it widely rumored on Wall Street but that he also had information from "someone well placed" at FINRA.[8] The fact that this allegation did not send shock waves throughout the financial press strongly suggests that the media was selective in pursuing leads while providing protection to those on Wall Street and in Washington. FINRA strongly denied this specific charge, which only served to highlight its lack of comment on the balance of the claims, especially those addressing its timely liquidation of ARS.

The discovery process for this complaint and the subsequent courtroom drama read like a riveting expose into how Wall Street operated and what exactly its primary self-regulatory organization was doing just prior to the market meltdown. While this case began to work its way into and through the legal system, FINRA did not sit idly by. Believing that the best defense was a good offense, FINRA undertook an aggressive marketing campaign, including time on the airwaves of major market radio stations. It also launched a self-review of its own oversight of both the Madoff and Stanford Financial scandals.[9] Despite reports that there was a reluctance within FINRA's board to release the self-review, the analysis provided little meaningful new information as to how both of these scams could have escaped the attention of the regulator. In fact, FINRA's self-review of its oversight of the Madoff scam largely limited it to a period going back only as far as 2003. And its own extensive relationships with Bernie Madoff and his family members were little more than a footnote.

Critics, including me, opined that a self-review of a self-regulatory organization was worth little more than the paper on which it was printed. Where was FINRA's overseer, the SEC, and why wasn't it pushing for greater transparency? The answer, of course, was that the SEC was licking its own wounds from embarrassing shortcomings on both these fronts. Be mindful that the new head of the SEC, Mary Schapiro, came directly from FINRA. If she were to hold the SRO accountable, she would have been shining the light upon herself. What about Congress? They held some perfunctory hearings to show how tough they were with the SEC, but did not even bother to call FINRA on the carpet. Investor outrage grew ever stronger.

While the Amerivet case worked its way through preliminary hearings and subsequent legal challenges, Johnson took his fight directly to the members of FINRA at its 2010 annual meeting. In an effort entitled the "Truth, Transparency, and Accountability Initiative," Johnson laid out much of what was detailed in the Amerivet complaint plus other points of conflict that were enveloping FINRA. Despite limited coverage by the media, the voices of FINRA's member firms resonated loudly throughout the industry, and the results of the voting on Johnson's initiative were an unqualified rout of the intransigent self-regulator:

In an extraordinary repudiation of a securities industry self-regulator, at the August 12th Annual Meeting two-thirds or more of FINRA members approved these seven common sense reforms many of which similar organizations have in place:

- Compensation for FINRA's top ten most highly paid employees should be reported regularly in the annual report (83 percent support);
- Management's relationships with Bernie Madoff and his family should be independently investigated (68 percent support);

- FINRA investment transactions should be disclosed to members and the public (76 percent support);
- FINRA Board of Governors meetings should be held in the "sunshine" open to the public (77 percent support);
- Members should have a "say on pay" for the top five compensated FINRA employees (72 percent supported);
- An independent private inspector general for FINRA should be appointed (67 percent support);
- All IRS correspondence on management's demonstrably false claims of a $35,000 ceiling on payments to NASD members related to its merger with NYSE to form FINRA should be released (70 percent supported).[10]

Amerivet counsel, Jon Cuneo, jumped to draw attention to these votes with a strong public pronouncement. "To avoid the appearance of concealing facts and obstructionism on all the matters addressed by the members' proxy votes, FINRA's Board of Governors should immediately adopt the recommendations overwhelmingly approved by its membership."[11]

Yet FINRA's management was nonplussed and responded with mere lip service; chairman and CEO Richard Ketchum and lead board governor Richard Brueckner inspired little confidence in the membership when they declared that the votes were non-binding and would be reviewed by FINRA's Board of Governors at its next meeting.

In due course, Ketchum informed industry representatives that the regulator would provide a degree of transparency on issues of compensation and investment management. On the other hot-button topics of greater transparency at the board level, the relationship with Madoff, the need for an independent private inspector general, and an investigation of the merger process that initially formed FINRA, he provided little of meaningful substance.

Throughout this time, I received messages from small broker-dealers around the country who were unwilling to speak publicly against FINRA for fear of retribution. One individual at a smaller firm wrote me, "There has been plenty of publicity about the goings on inside FINRA. 4,000 small BDs are all aware of it and feel the effects. That said, nothing can be done to change the environment. What is wrong with this picture? How far up the food chain are the payoffs going?"

The growing anxiety among investors and smaller FINRA member firms resonated with the Alliance for Economic Stability (AES), a nonpartisan economic policy organization that encourages regulatory policies that protect savings and investments. The AES tried to pull back the FINRA cloak by imploring the Financial Crisis Inquiry Commission to investigate Wall Street's "private police." That call also went into Washington's black hole of silence.

With all the public pressure for greater transparency mounting, FINRA was forced to abandon its deft style of public defense in favor of a hard line. FINRA spokesman Herb Perone, shortly after the Amerivet complaint was filed, stated unequivocally, "Our records are not open for public examination."[12] If investors, member firms, and public policy organizations could not compel FINRA to open its books so we could gain a real understanding as to how Wall Street really worked, the judicial process was our only hope.

Recall that FINRA is a private organization. The fact that this private organization is industry-funded, not for profit, and reports to the SEC does not change the fact that it is private. Yet the FINRA defense rested upon a privilege typically accorded only to government agencies, that is, FINRA asserted that in the case of *Amerivet*

Securities v. FINRA, it was afforded absolute immunity so as not to be subject to lawsuits and complaints such as this.

But in truth, this privilege of absolute immunity is supposed to apply only to issues that fall under its regulatory umbrella. For cases that are not considered to be of a regulatory nature, FINRA is not afforded this benefit and is supposed to operate under the laws of the land.

Even in the face of this steep challenge, Amerivet and its attorneys fought on and pursued the case based upon the premise that they were not looking for monetary compensation but merely proper regulatory governance. The FINRA defense, not surprisingly, moved for dismissal based upon the premise of absolute immunity. Amerivet's pursuit gained a minor victory when the Honorable John M. Mott, associate judge in the Superior Court of the District of Columbia Civil Division, denied FINRA's motion for dismissal. Mott wrote an opinion acknowledging that selected aspects of this case filed against FINRA did fall under its regulatory umbrella and were thus protected by the privilege of immunity; however, the judge also offered that whether other aspects were regulatory in nature or not could only be determined by an inspection of FINRA's books and records.

That partial victory provided temporary sustenance for the plaintiff, but it did not lead to ultimate victory for Amerivet and those who cared to learn more about FINRA and the culture within this organization that had egregiously failed to uphold its mandate to protect investors. The case was ultimately settled out of court, with plaintiff and attorneys unable to comment on the settlement. The press provided little to no coverage.

Life on Wall Street went on.

The resounding lack of truth and transparency in the Amerivet case brought me back to my own appearance on "America's Nightly Scoreboard" when the case was first filed. The host, David Asman, inquired of me, "Larry, it goes to the point that a lot of people are looking from the outside at what goes on inside in Wall Street and Washington. It's that Wall Street–Washington nexus. They see all these folks kind of related with each other. The SEC related with FINRA, and related with NASD. You look at Mary Schapiro's career and you see that. They can miss things because they're only talking to each other."

I responded, "I think the term there is *incestuous*."[13]

With the passage of time, the benefit of hindsight, and the preponderance of evidence, American taxpayers can finally conclude that a regulatory cover of absolute immunity combined with little meaningful transparency added up to a license to steal—for Wall Street and Washington alike.

SEVEN
IMMUNITY

Well I think there's no question that we need far more transparency throughout the regulatory environment, both for those regulated and those doing the regulation. That, I think, is a very clear proposition.

—Former SEC chair Harvey Pitt,
America's Nightly Scoreboard,
Fox Business, September 3, 2009

THE WORLD OF PROFESSIONAL SPORTS HAS BEEN TAINTED over the last number of years as leading athletes admitted to using anabolic steroids and other performance-enhancing drugs. Cheating scandals have certainly tarnished the reputations of those involved and damaged the public trust in the institution. Yet, by and large, the games have gone on.

One scandal, though, rocked the world of professional basketball to its core. The revelation that veteran NBA referee Tim Donaghy was gambling on games and feeding inside information to gamblers made the use of performance-enhancing drugs look like child's play. League commissioner David Stern called this travesty the "most serious situation and worst situation I have ever experienced" in his tenure at the post.[1] And the fans felt it too—the Donaghy scandal struck at the very heart and integrity of the game. There's no quicker way to alienate fans than to suggest that the level playing field has been compromised.

Wall Street is often compared to the world of competitive sports. The fast-paced, high-stress environment attracts plenty of college athletes and other competitive types. No doubt that will to win drives some to bend or break the rules of the game. Most people on Wall Street dislike this element, but they're certainly aware it exists. How would Wall Street participants—employees and investors alike—react to a Tim Donaghy-type experience in their midst? Certainly, many investors have been highly critical of the Wall Street referees, who have not upheld and enforced the letter of the law in a vigorous fashion.

What would actually dissuade the Wall Street referees from breaking the rules? Transparency is the great disinfectant. Yes, that same transparency that was shown to be seriously lacking in the *Amerivet Securities v. FINRA* case. The same transparency that many in Washington are more than happy to promote on the stump, but are reluctant to practice when truly needed. The same transparency that is too often addressed only in arcane details buried deep in the fine print of offering documents. The same transparency that former SEC chair Harvey Pitt extolled, yet which was sorely lacking in his own organization while he was in command.

Amerivet—including its unanswered questions regarding FINRA's liquidation of ARS and an investment with Madoff—provided strong evidence of the lack of meaningful transparency within FINRA, and an accompanying meaningful lack of investor protection as a result. Amerivet attorney Jon Cuneo summed up his findings as follows: "FINRA is the largest private regulator for all securities firms doing business in the United States, yet it is run like a secret society. . . . The organization claims to promote transparency in the financial industry, while simultaneously fighting a battle to hide very basic information from its members and the public."[2]

As damning as the *Amerivet* case was to the premise of meaningful transparency and upstanding, unbiased regulation, it paled in comparison to one brought by Standard Investment Chartered—on behalf of itself and all other FINRA members—against FINRA and select FINRA defendants, including Mary Schapiro, *Standard Investment Chartered v. Financial Industry Regulatory Authority*. That complaint was followed by another from Benchmark Financial, *Benchmark Financial Services v. Financial Industry Regulatory Authority*, making largely the same claims.

These two complaints painted Mary Schapiro and other FINRA executives as part and parcel of the Wall Street cronyism—in effect, suggesting they were the Tim Donaghys of the financial world. The complaints also impugned the very integrity of the documents utilized in the merger of the two regulatory organizations that formed FINRA in 2007.

FINRA was formed as the result of a merger of the NASD, founded in 1939, and the regulatory arm of the New York Stock Exchange. Mergers and acquisitions are a large part of Wall Street's business. The takeovers and consolidations of various enterprises are core to the spirit and practice of capitalism. The success or failure of mergers and acquisitions rests upon a host of variables, including the melding of disparate cultures, the ability to develop business plans and then execute them, and the acceptance of the merger by the marketplace. The outcomes on all these fronts are often predicated on the inputs provided by both entities involved in the transaction. Many mergers fail or underperform because one or both sides didn't properly evaluate the array of intangibles—or the underlying financials—involved. That is also part of capitalism. What should not be part of capitalism is a purposeful omission or deception in the merger documentation from the outset.

To consummate a merger, the shareholders of each organization are typically allowed to vote on whether or not they support the merger. The SEC requires every company to provide its shareholders with a proxy statement, which is a document containing pertinent information necessary to evaluate the merger itself. Topics covered in the proxy might include proposals for new additions to the board of directors, information on directors' salaries, information on bonus and options plans for directors, and any declarations made by company management. The financials and the proxy are usually reviewed by auditors prior to being disseminated for review by the shareholders. To fully understand the essence of the merger that formed FINRA, and the central issues of the Benchmark and Standard Investment complaints, we need to follow the money.

The NYSE was founded in the late 1700s and grew to be an exceptionally powerful institution. The growth of the exchange and the accompanying growth of the daily flow of trading led to the birth of other regional exchanges. Another New York–based exchange, the American Stock Exchange, was born in the early 1900s under the name the New York Curb Exchange. Despite the growth in other exchanges, the real power remained with the NYSE and the individuals and firms that ran it.

The NYSE was primarily known for its exchange-related activities, but it also had a regulatory arm that worked in sync with its market-making operations. This regulatory arm monitored the primarily larger broker-dealers that were members of the NYSE. Juxtaposed with the NYSE was the NASD, founded in 1939 for the purpose of regulating non-exchange related trading activity in what was known as the over-the-counter market. With exchange trading showing no sign of letting up and with the national economic landscape expanding, the individuals running the NASD took a revolutionary approach to competing with the NYSE in the trading arena by launching what was essentially a computer bulletin board. Initially known as the National Association of Securities Dealers Automated Quotations (NASDAQ), it grew by focusing almost exclusively on technology companies. As the tech space grew, the NASDAQ grew right along with it. The exchange was initially unpopular with many brokerage firms because it brought increased liquidity and narrower trading spreads into the marketplace. Its appealing slogan was, "The stock market for the next hundred years." And one of its founders was Bernie Madoff.

The NASDAQ quickly grew into a thriving enterprise, but due to concerns about conflicts of interest between a market-making enterprise and a regulator (imagine that!), the NASD decided to spin it off in 2000 into a for-profit enterprise via a private placement offering. Unlike a public offering of shares, a private placement is a sale of securities in an entity such as the NASDAQ to a relatively small number of select investors. This transaction, and subsequent offerings of NASDAQ stock and warrants, looked to raise a sum of $1.5 billion for the majority shareholders of this exchange, those being the owners and management of the thousands of small, medium, and large member firms of the NASD.

In similar fashion, the NYSE transitioned from a not-for-profit to a for-profit enterprise in 2005 as a result of a merger with an electronic exchange founded in 1994, known as Archipelago Holdings.

With the two largest exchanges becoming for profit and increasingly electronic in nature, the landscape on Wall Street was changing rapidly. Yet the regulatory landscape remained very much the same. The NYSE regulatory arm focused mostly on the exchange activities of the larger broker-dealers. The NASD monitored the over-the-counter activities of the many thousands of large, medium, and small broker-dealers. Consolidating these operations, in the name of capturing synergies and mitigating overlaps, was alluring. Then CEO of Goldman Sachs and eventual Secretary of the Treasury Henry Paulson had been lobbying for just such a single authority on Wall Street since 2000. The eventual merger, completed in 2007, was touted as forming a single regulator best positioned to facilitate the growth and development of our economy and markets, while simultaneously maximizing investor protection:

> "The creation of FINRA is the most significant modernization of the self-regulatory regime in decades," said Mary L. Schapiro, Chief Executive Officer of FINRA. "With investor protection and market integrity as our overarching objectives, FINRA will be an investor-focused and more streamlined regulator that is better suited to the complexity and competitiveness of today's global capital markets. By eliminating overlapping regulation and establishing a uniform set of rules placing oversight responsibility in a single organization, we will enhance investor protection while increasing the competitiveness of our financial markets."
>
> "On behalf of the entire organization," Schapiro continued, "I want to thank the teams from both NASD and NYSE Regulation, who have worked tirelessly over the past seven months to turn this vision into reality. As the FINRA team moves forward with its integration plans, safeguarding investors and the integrity of the markets will continue to be our top priorities."[3]

Conveniently left out of Schapiro's message were the specifics of the "work" those teams undertook to make the vision a reality. What about the large pool of capital from the private placement offering of the NASDAQ, still sitting within the NASD? Those funds remained the property of the member firms. How would they be handled post-merger? The specifics of the merger initially received little attention within the mainstream financial media, but the *Corporate Crime Reporter* highlighted the following allegation: "FINRA member firms are due more than the $35,000 they received as part of the 2007 merger between National Association of Securities Dealers (NASD) and the regulatory arm of the New York Stock Exchange—a merger that resulted in the creation of FINRA. At the time of the merger negotiations, NASD told its members that because it was a non-profit, the most it could pay each firm was $35,000. But in March 2007, the Internal Revenue Service (IRS) issued a private letter ruling which indicated that in fact NASD could pay a lot more than $35,000. How much more is a secret."[4]

Here we go again. The shroud of opacity surrounding this organization now had real consequences. While the NASD's management informed its members that the $35,000 payment would be generated by future savings from efficiencies within the consolidated regulatory agency, plaintiffs in a subsequent lawsuit maintained that the true source of the funds were misappropriations of the members' equity in the organization.

Many legal disputes ultimately hinge on differences of opinion—gray areas. These complaints did not. For instance, regarding when the road show for the merger of the NASD and regulatory arm of the NYSE occurred, Mary Schapiro herself stated in the NASD's annual report, "In 2006, I traveled across the country with senior NASD executives to encourage members to vote on the plan for regulatory consolidation with NYSE Member Regulation, and to discuss its merits. We visited 26 cities, and met with more than 800 firms face-to-face."[5] The proxy statement itself was dated December 14, 2006.

Yet, "the IRS did not issue a formal ruling on the payment to members until March 13, 2007."[6] Wait a second. Schapiro and team in 2006 are promoting the merger and informing NASD member firms as to what sort of payout they would receive for approving the merger, and the IRS had not even issued a ruling until March 2007? How does that work?

Let's take a look at the *Second Amended Complaint Brought on Behalf of Standard Investment Chartered et al. v. FINRA, NYSE Group, Mary L. Schapiro, et al.:*

Centrally, the FINRA Defendants falsely stated that, according to the Internal Revenue Service ("IRS"), $35,000 per NASD Member (or approximately $175 million) was the maximum amount that could be paid to the Members. In actuality, according to the IRS Private Letter Ruling, NASD/FINRA could have paid NASD Members an additional [redacted figure] per NASD Member form or [redacted figure] in the aggregate.[7]

The complaint also alleged:

IRS did not limit the payment to member firms to $35,000 as NASD and its officials insisted. NASD Board Minutes demonstrate that the Board discussed the $35,000 limit stating, "regardless of the amount agreed upon, it was paramount that the figure not be subject to negotiation."[8]

If the IRS stated that the payment to member firms was not limited to $35,000, but NASD (FINRA) representatives maintained that the $35,000 figure was the maximum allowed by the IRS, then this conflict was no mild misunderstanding.

While the *Benchmark/Standard Investment* complaint worked its way through the courts, one great mystery was what exactly were the figures that had been redacted in the complaint? How much would the IRS have really allowed FINRA to pay out to its member firms, and, as such, just how much of the members' equity was misappropriated? The mainstream media finally picked up on the explosiveness of the charges. Acting in the public interest, the *New York Times, Barron's,* and *Bloomberg News* beseeched the court to release the unredacted documents so as to solve the mystery and test the accuracy and integrity of the valuation claimed by Schapiro and the other defendants.

The unredacted documents were never released, but in court plaintiffs' counsel directly addressed this "big money" question. *Bloomberg*'s Susan Antilla and Jesse Westbrook reported:

> NASD, which became Finra after merging with the New York Stock Exchange's oversight unit, could pay "something" from $70,000 to $111,000, Jonathan Cuneo, the lawyer for Benchmark Financial Services Inc. and Standard Investment Chartered Inc., said yesterday at a hearing, citing confidential Internal Revenue Service documents. NASD told brokerages in 2006 that IRS policy limited the payments to $35,000.
>
> There is a "substantial difference between what NASD said" and what the IRS would have allowed, Cuneo, an attorney at Cuneo Gilbert & LaDuca LLP, said during the hearing in U.S. District Court in Manhattan. . . .
>
> Cuneo's estimate is based on information in a confidential ruling the IRS sent to NASD that Finra has sought to keep secret. He commented during a hearing in New York on Finra's request to dismiss the lawsuit.[9]

If Cuneo's information was correct, it would mean that Mary Schapiro and her band of cronies took their traveling troupe to 26 cities and visited more than 800 firms and put forth a wildly inaccurate estimate, the size of which they may not have known at the time but ultimately had a dollar value between approximately $178 million and $387 million. The potential difference is the gap between the $35,000 for 5,100 firms ($178.5 million total) suggested by the defendants and the figures Cuneo alleged were actually proposed by the IRS of $70,000 to $111,000 per member firm. With 5,100 member firms, the IRS estimates would have equated to gross totals between $356 million and $566 million.

These figures are important, and not simply because a regulator would have sold itself out for its own financial gain and that of a number of large banks. Far more importantly, they would represent a payoff made to the industry's self-regulatory organization as it compromised its mandate to protect the interests of investors.

As plaintiffs' counsel emphatically asserted, every fact and appearance unearthed to this point indicated that the merger forming FINRA was delivered "through an inaccurate and deceptive proxy statement and solicitation process."[10] The integrity of proxy statements on Wall Street is supposed to be sacrosanct, yet here, in no uncertain words, the counsel for Benchmark and Standard Investment called Schapiro and her colleagues a pack of liars.

The alleged deceit went far deeper than the egregious misrepresentation of a potentially large sum of money. The complaint also alleged that one of the defense's central claims—that the powers of the SEC itself were poised to weigh in on behalf of the NASD—was patently false. According to the complaint, even basic rules of accounting were violated when FINRA "omitted the material fact that the Members stood to receive over $300,000 per firm if NASD were to be dissolved and replaced with a new SRO and/or if NYSE were the surviving SRO."[11] Additionally, plaintiffs' counsel maintained that FINRA did not receive a "Fairness Opinion from a qualified and reputable expert as to the economic fairness of the Transaction and the Member payments under all the circumstances" prior to the issuance of the proxy statement and Special Meeting of NASD Members to approve the transaction.[12]

The NASD/FINRA defendants are charged with promoting full and proper disclosures in the name of investor protection; if the charges alleged by plaintiffs are correct, however, they seemed to conveniently forget those virtues while embracing obfuscation, scare tactics, and outright lies in their pursuit of completing this merger. Not exactly the principles of good governance, but often the most effective way to entrench power and retain large financial gains.

Aside from the institutional benefits accruing to the regulator, plaintiffs' counsel also alleged personal benefits accruing to the individual defendants, as they "abused their positions of trust and authority, misrepresented key facts repeatedly, orally and in writing, and sacrificed the interests of the Plaintiff and members of the Class ("Members") so that the Officer Defendants could line their pockets."[13] Not a lot left to interpretation there.

To this point the complaint centered on benefits directed to the regulator itself and the individual defendants. But if FINRA were truly in bed with the industry, the large Wall Street firms must also somehow benefit from this merger. Plaintiffs' counsel zeroed in on this point. Unbeknownst to all those outside of Wall Street—and most inside the industry as well—the proxy utilized for this merger omitted the material fact that NYSE and the large Wall Street banks "stood to reap enormous benefits from the Transaction at the expense of the NASD Members [i.e., primarily small firms] who were not also members of NYSE."[14]

This single sentence speaks volumes to what Harry Markopolos meant when stating that FINRA was "in bed with the industry." Plaintiffs' counsel is highlighting that the larger broker-dealers on Wall Street (Goldman Sachs, J.P. Morgan, Morgan Stanley, et al.)

accrued "enormous benefits" from the merger that formed FINRA: the elimination of a source of regulatory oversight at the NYSE and access to the assets of the NASD, which could be diverted to offset their own costs for the SRO system.

In one fell swoop, the firms that dominate the Wall Street landscape benefited—in terms of both oversight and cost—from the elimination of one of their primary regulators. And the fact that they're showered with these gifts by none other than the regulators themselves is particularly enlightening. Not that Wall Street did not enjoy a whole host of other "benefits" within the realm of self-regulation, but with all of the pleasures from this merger alone, one can only imagine what other favors were exchanged over the years.

While the large firms benefited, the little ones paid. The approximately 4,900 small and medium-size NASD members saw their equity redirected for the benefit of the big guys. Markopolos was right. FINRA was in bed with the industry.

The implications of this reality may not be expressly evident to investors and consumers. But in my mind, it's the primary reason we've been unable to guarantee basic protection for investors navigating the markets. In my strong opinion, this transaction and this incestuous relationship between FINRA and Wall Street are the answers to the single greatest question emanating from our economic crisis: Where were the regulators and what were they doing? They were in bed with the industry, but investors were the ones really getting screwed.

While investors suffered the pain of loss and anxiety, FINRA once again invoked its claim of absolute immunity in an attempt to dismiss the complaint. The immunity typically granted to governmental regulatory agencies, however, was supposed to apply only to regulatory pursuits. This merger struck most observers as a financial transaction to consolidate regulators, not simply a regulatory matter per se.

If the information and evidence provided to this point were not convincing enough of FINRA's and the industry's incestuous and complicit conspiratorial behavior, then let's pull back the blanket just a little bit further. In what might only be compared to a vindictive spouse caught red-handed with a paramour, FINRA gave the following shameless defense: "In the nearly two years that several NASD Members have repeatedly challenged the representation about the $35,000 cap in court and administrative proceedings, the NASD has responded by arguing: (a) that it and its officials are immune from suit; (b) that the courts have no jurisdiction to hear the challenges made by Plaintiff and other Members; (c) that the state common law issues raised by this action are SEC matters; (d) that the Members have no right to know whether they were told the truth; and (e) that the truth should be kept secret from the public. But they have never denied that the IRS approved an amount payable to Members that was much higher than $35,000!"[15]

"The truth should be kept secret from the public." So much for transparency if the above-quoted passage accurately reflected FINRA's position. Indeed, if FINRA believes that the truth should be selectively kept from the public, who knows what else we don't know?

One of FINRA's members was strongly suspicious of the FINRA defendants' motivations on the road shows and said as much in writing to me, but the words are very much directed to the FINRA Board:

Disenchanted, February 13, 2010

When is the truth going to prevail? It was quite obvious during the road shows that there were many "untruths" being told. The

Board needs to open the doors and consider all allegations, not just compensation.

I guess that since there are no Supervisory procedure manuals or AML (anti-money laundering) procedures or SEC 3012 or 2011 filings, there is nothing for them to look at. After all, during an audit, those are the most important things. Paying attention to whistleblowers, or looking for phony trading is not important, especially if you are one of the good old boys. Stop picking on the little guy. . . . A good place to start would be with the executives (past and present) of FINRA and then work down the ladder.[16]

At the same time in early 2010, while FINRA's defense counsel was claiming immunity, the Financial Crisis Inquiry Commission (FCIC) began to hold hearings to determine the root causes of the crisis. Who was one of the first individuals to provide testimony to this nonpartisan body charged with investigating the past so as to determine the causes of our economic crisis and subsequent market meltdown? None other than Mary Schapiro.

Her counsel was in New York, and received little attention or exposure while proclaiming immunity for FINRA. Schapiro was in Washington and put forth an opening statement to the FCIC that referenced the SEC more than 100 times. She referenced her former employer, the NASD (FINRA), once. So much for delving into the past. Was the topic of self-regulation on Wall Street somehow off limits to those on the FCIC and in Congress, as well? Very possibly.

Schapiro's opening statement went on to reference disclosure, or the need for greater disclosure, 27 times. She referenced transparency, or the need for greater transparency, 13 times.[17] At the same time she had to know full well that her counsel was stonewalling the very pursuit of disclosure and transparency on behalf of plaintiffs' counsel in the *Benchmark, Standard Investment,* and *Amerivet* complaints.

With the truth in short supply on the financial regulatory front, this case did serve to unite an otherwise disparate collection of individuals and public policy groups. Many from both the Tea Party and Occupy movement have called for an open window into Wall Street regulation. As the *Benchmark/Standard Investment* complaints worked their way through the courts, groups with widely differing points of view on most topics joined forces to call for accountability and transparency in this case. *Investment News* captured their sentiments:

"The case presents a situation where a quasi-governmental entity is abusing its power," said Ilya Shapiro, a constitutional lawyer at the libertarian Cato Institute, which joined with the Competitive Enterprise Institute in filing an amicus brief on behalf of Standard.

"Our legal interest is really to make government accountable," he said.

"There's a larger principle at stake: to what extent state actors can be held accountable," said William Anderson, one of Standard's lawyers at Cuneo Gilbert & LaDuca LLP. "That's why the various groups have weighed in" with amicus briefs, he said.

"We're concerned about the court's overextension of immunity" to private organizations, said Scott Michelman, a staff attorney at the Public Citizen Litigation Group, which, together with Consumer Action, The Project On Government Oversight and the U.S. Public Interest Research Group, also is urging the Supreme Court to take the case.

"In this case, immunity has been extended to private corporate actors . . . in a way that could prevent corporate accountability," he said.

Standard and its supporters dispute the earlier court findings that NASD's proxy and merger were "incident to" its regulatory activities and thus protected.

The Cato Institute argues that such a standard "would be the equivalent of shielding a judge who ran down a pedestrian on his way to the courthouse simply because his travel there eventually will lead to his exercising judicial power."[18]

Clearly Wall Street and Washington had little real interest in embracing the virtues of accountability and transparency—let alone integrity—within the world of financial regulation.

Meanwhile, the media had picked up on just enough of the FINRA and SEC stories that the American public finally began to understand what was so rank within the financial regulatory system. Their suspicions hardened with the mortgage fraud scandal, the decline of MF Global, and the dubious high-frequency trading. Naked short selling was a distant memory. The manipulation of Libor had yet to come front and center.

Who looked to aerate the smell surrounding Wall Street regulation? None other than consumer advocate, securities attorney, and *Benchmark/Standard* counsel Richard Greenfield. In the course of a public interview I had with Greenfield, he left little to interpretation: "Both agencies [SEC and FINRA] were effectively Keystone Cops . . . they were running around in circles and didn't know what they were doing. I would have expected more from the SEC, which has a bigger budget and far greater competence than the NASD or what is now known as FINRA, where the mindset has never been on major league enforcement. It has always been on relatively picayune broker-dealer violations and even then the violations were very much more technical in nature than they were real. The 'Big Boys' always seem to get away with murder."[19] Turning specifically to the topic of the *Benchmark* and *Standard Investment* complaints, Green-field further exposed the defendants: "We were able to get discovery, that is document presentation from the NASD, very early on. Many of these documents were produced under a confidentiality order; in other words, the NASD wouldn't produce them unless they could be kept confidential, i.e., not in the public record. These documents showed unequivocally that the NASD defendants lied to the members of the NASD. Blatantly, unequivocally, you can't put any coloration on it, you can't say they were negligent. They intentionally lied. The lies are repeated over and over in a proxy statement. They are repeated in road shows taken all around the country."[20]

Not pulling any punches there, although given the confidentiality demand made by the defendants, it may never be possible to verify the accuracy of these charges.

Yet in a manner that seems all too consistent with those who had hoped to keep the pedophilia scandal buried within the Catholic Church, the NASD defendants maintained that "its confidential internal documents also raise privacy concerns and their disclosure may have unintended consequences on the nation's securities markets."[21] Talk about scare tactics. In so many words, NASD counsel warned that the markets would be spooked by this financial, political, and regulatory ménage à trois if the blankets were ever to be pulled back. In the process, NASD counsel seems to admit just how powerful and damning this evidence truly is. In the end, obviously, you can't expect the police to protect you when they're aiding and abetting the breaking and entering of your house. Keep in mind that while the defendants in this case were working so diligently in late 2006 and early 2007 to complete this merger, our economy and markets were moving ever closer to the edge of the cliff.

The defendants in these complaints were FINRA, the NYSE Group (including all the major Wall Street banks), FINRA board member Richard F. Brueckner, FINRA General Counsel T. Grant Callery, FINRA Executive Vice President and CFO Todd Diganci, FINRA Executive Vice President Howard M. Schloss, and former FINRA CEO and the chair of the SEC during President Obama's first term Mary L. Schapiro.

The case was ultimately appealed all the way to the United States Supreme Court, which in early 2012 chose not to hear it.

EIGHT
FAKE SECURITY

SIPC is giving investors a false sense of security, and that is dangerous for those who have been led to believe that they can trust the system.

—Ron Stein, President, Network for Investor Action
and Protection, September 23, 2010

RISK IS A CENTRAL FEATURE OF A STRONG CAPITALIST system. Most people are generally risk-averse. Others with real vision and a willingness to embrace risk have precipitated the launch of a wide array of new products and the opening of new markets. American ingenuity is ultimately fueled by the risk takers in our society. That said, real success is often much less a function of pure appetite for risk than an ability for effectively managing risks.

On Wall Street and everywhere else, truly effective risk management is predicated on a number of variables. Within an organization, risk management relies on robust systems to capture and process information in a timely fashion, as well as strong managers to monitor potential pitfalls while instituting rigorous ethics and values.

In the marketplace of products and ideas, risk management depends on legal entities enacting and regulators upholding meaningful rules of the road. Effective regulation is essential to maintain fair and balanced markets and mitigate the potential of loss. Even with best practices in place, though, losses happen. It's inevitable in any capitalist system. Hence the other risk management tool widely employed in both our professional and personal lives—insurance.

While historical data suggests that risk-sharing arrangements go back as far as the Phoenician era, the principles of modern day insurance stem from the Great Fire of London in 1666. While the loss of life from this accidentally caused conflagration was minimal, it consumed close to 80 percent of the city over the course of five days, destroyed countless businesses, and left approximately 100,000 people homeless. Out of the ashes was born the need for meaningful insurance.

Since those early days in London, the insurance industry has grown exponentially to cover almost every risk imaginable. Interestingly, though, insurance did not find its way into the banking system here in the United States until the 1930s, and specifically into the financial system and Wall Street until 1970.

The Great Depression brought about many changes in America, including the initiation of meaningful financial regulation. At the same time, the Federal Deposit Insurance Corporation was launched in 1933 in response to the thousands of bank failures that occurred in the 1920s and early 1930s. When unveiling the FDIC, President Franklin Delano Roosevelt addressed the nation and said:

> We had a bad banking situation. Some of our bankers had shown themselves either incompetent or dishonest in their handling of the people's funds. They had used the money entrusted to them in speculations and unwise loans. This was of course not true in the vast majority of our banks but it was true in enough of them to shock the people for a time into a sense of insecurity and to

put them into a frame of mind where they did not differentiate, but seemed to assume that the acts of a comparative few had tainted them all. It was the Government's job to straighten out this situation and do it as quickly as possible—and the job is being performed.

I do not promise you that every bank will be reopened or that individual losses will not be suffered, but there will be no losses that possibly could be avoided; and there would have been more and greater losses had we continued to drift. I can even promise you salvation for some at least of the sorely pressed banks. We shall be engaged not merely in reopening sound banks but in the creation of sound banks through reorganization. It has been wonderful to me to catch the note of confidence from all over the country. I can never be sufficiently grateful to the people for the loyal support they have given me in their acceptance of the judgment that has dictated our course, even though all of our processes may not have seemed clear to them.

After all there is an element in the readjustment of our financial system more important than currency, more important than gold, and that is the confidence of the people. Confidence and courage are the essentials of success in carrying out our plan.[1]

The parallels to today are plain. Back then, Congress did try to address similar concerns of confidence within the brokerage industry, but with little success.

"Before 1938, little protection existed for customers of a bankrupt stockbroker unless they could trace cash and securities held by failed stockbrokers. In 1938 Congress enacted section 60(e) of the Bankruptcy Act creating a single and separate fund concept to minimize losses to customers by giving them priority over claims of general creditors. . . . Because the fund was normally inadequate, however, customer losses continued."[2] This inadequacy of funds in 1938 would serve as a precursor to a similar lack of funds 70 years later.

Congress's 1938 attempt to provide a means of insurance for investors was unsuccessful. It was not until another boom and subsequent bust on Wall Street that meaningful investor protection via an insurance fund was finally established. A contraction befell Wall Street in the late 1960s amid the industry's inability to properly process a surge in trading volume; this precipitated the ultimate bankruptcy of a number of brokerages and the eventual enactment of the Securities Investor Protection Act (SIPA). This new legislation was intended to restore confidence in the system for the benefit of the industry and investors: "Congress designed the SIPA to apportion responsibility for carrying out the various goals of the legislation to several groups. Among them are the Securities and Exchange Commission, various securities industry self-regulatory organizations, and the Securities Investor Protection Corporation (SIPC)."[3]

The SIPC is much like FINRA in that it is an industry-funded, nongovernmental, not-for-profit corporation. It was created so that "when a brokerage firm is closed due to bankruptcy or other financial difficulties and customer assets are missing, SIPC steps in as quickly as possible and, within certain limits, works to return customers' cash, stock and other securities, and other customer property."[4]

Insurance against the risk of a securities brokerage house going bankrupt may seem irrelevant during periods of calm. However, it is during those periods when executives managing entities such as the FDIC and SIPC should be planning for periods of stress and instability. We witness little of this prudent foresight in remarks made by SIPC Chair Armando Bucelo in SIPC's 2007 annual report, just a year before the tsunami that overwhelmed our markets and our nation. As the financial hurricane centered on Wall Street was gaining strength, Bucelo and his team at SIPC displayed the same benign blindness as their fellow agencies.

> The year 2007 saw an event which has never previously occurred in the 37 year history of SIPC. During the year, SIPC was not called upon to initiate a customer protection proceeding for any SIPC member brokerage firm. Indeed, in the four year period from 2004 to 2007, SIPC was called upon to initiate proceedings for a total of only six brokerage firms. This is the lowest number of new proceedings during any four year period in our corporate history. As I have mentioned before in previous Annual Reports, I attribute this extraordinary result to the vigilance of the Securities and Exchange Commission, the Financial Industry Regulatory Authority, and the state regulators, who assure customers that their assets are properly segregated and that brokerage firms maintain capital adequacy.
>
> SIPC's Board of Directors is constantly concerned that SIPC has sufficient resources to deal with any foreseeable circumstance. At year end, the SIPC Fund stood at an all time high. The low level of brokerage failures over the last few years has allowed our assets to grow, since those funds were not needed to satisfy new customer claims. Notwithstanding the record level of our financial resources, the Board chartered a new study of SIPC's capital adequacy by an outside consultant. I am pleased to report that the consultants have concluded that the size of the SIPC Fund is sufficient to meet SIPC's mission. The probability that the Fund will be exhausted in a one year period is very small.[5]

Bucelo's lead statement in SIPC's 2007 annual report was released on April 30, 2008. Clearly, reports of that sort are written long before they are published, but I'll bet Bucelo would have liked to have rewritten his rosy assessment. Bear Stearns effectively failed and was taken over by J.P. Morgan on March 16, 2008, a full six weeks prior to the release of the SIPC report. Bear was the initial wave. The storm behind it brought the demise of Lehman Brothers and laid to waste Bucelo's laudatory assessment of SIPC, the SEC, FINRA, and other financial regulators. Suddenly, these supposed protectors of the public interest seemed somnolent—or worse.

Bucelo certainly should have known that the performance of any insurance product or its provider is not to be judged during a period of calm, but rather during a period of stress. Those running such insurance companies or funds are hired for their foresight, not hindsight.

With the demise of Lehman and then Bernard Madoff Securities in late 2008, SIPC's projection that its fund would not be exhausted in a year was trashed. As investors thrashed about in the market meltdown, Madoff's victims wondered how the regulators could have failed them so badly. While answers to the regulatory failures were not quickly forthcoming, the immediate question for the Madoff investors was whether the SIPC stamp of protection on their Madoff brokerage statements meant anything.

SIPC reports up and through the SEC, so this life-changing question fell in the lap of none other than SEC chair Mary Schapiro in mid-2009. In the course of her testimony to the congressional Committee on Financial Services, Schapiro was asked by Congressman Gary Ackerman (D-NY), "Which investors are eligible for their SIPC insurance?" Schapiro hesitated, adjusted the microphone, and then replied, "It shouldn't be such a difficult issue but it is." She then went on to say, "The tragic truth is there is not enough money available to pay off all the customer claims."[6]

Countless Madoff investors—many of them senior citizens—were left near destitute, wondering how they might move forward with their lives. Wall Street and Washington knew they owed America answers as to what happened with Madoff. Would the victims—and America at large—ever get a satisfactory explanation of how Madoff perpetrated such a large scam for such a long time?

One leader within the Madoff investors' coalition knew full well that to get real answers, she'd have to dig into SIPC and other organizations. Attorney Helen Davis Chaitman provided endless hours of pro bono service to her fellow Madoff investors. Her efforts unearthed information on SIPC that was almost impossible to fathom.

Although SIPC is not a de facto insurance entity—but rather a nonprofit, nongovernmental membership corporation for the brokerage industry—in spirit and principle it acts as one. As with any entity of this sort, to determine whether SIPC had appropriate coverage, you must assess total overall exposures, funds available to pay claims, and premiums paid by those broker-dealers offering the SIPC stamp of protection. As we have learned, SIPC believed its fund at the end of 2007 was sufficient to cover potential claims. During this period, Wall Street was experiencing explosive growth.

Wall Street operates on leverage—that is, they use borrowed funds to run their operations. The ability to utilize increased leverage would allow the Wall Street banks and broker-dealers to borrow more funds, put more assets to work on their balance sheets, and generate greater revenue and returns, albeit with greater risk. Up until 2004, Wall Street was allowed by regulators to operate with a not insignificant 15 times leverage—in other words, they were required to hold one dollar of equity capital for every 15 dollars of assets on their books. In layman's terms, this would be the equivalent of putting down a deposit of approximately $6,500 on a home purchased for $100,000.

In the early years of the new millennium, Goldman Sachs CEO Henry Paulson led Wall Street's solicitation of the SEC to allow the industry to utilize much greater leverage by changing this net capital rule. Paulson and his pals ultimately prevailed, and the SEC allowed an alternative method of measuring net capital beginning in 2004. As defined by the SEC, this alternative standard allowed that a "broker or dealer shall not permit its net capital to be less than the greater of $250,000 or 2 percent of aggregate debit items."[7]

In other words, the large banks on Wall Street were now only required to put down $2,000 or thereabouts on that $100,000 home. One dollar of equity capital could now support a much larger balance sheet with much greater risk in the hope, and with the expectation, of generating much greater returns. And those banks took full advantage of this new freedom.

If an individual tripled the size of his home—with borrowed funds, nonetheless—the mortgage company would compel him to add a requisite amount of insurance. In similar fashion, if a business owner doubled or tripled the size and risk of his enterprise with borrowed funds, those lending the money would certainly inspect the business to make sure that sufficient insurance was in place to cover potential claims and loss. (Author's note: Post-crisis regulations now require the banks to increase their levels of equity capital in a fashion so as to decrease the amount of leverage and accompanying risk. This process remains anything but transparent and continues to produce endless debate regarding the fact that the "too big to fail" banks have only gotten bigger post-crisis.)

With the doubling and tripling of leverage on Wall Street, one might assume that SIPC was requiring bigger premiums from its Wall Street member firms to offset the increased risks. But of course, the Madoff fiasco—replete with SIPC stamps of protection on customer account statements—exposed that coverage as being of little value.

Even in 2007, a year when shareholders in Wall Street firms lost more than $80 billion in value, the five largest investment banks on Wall Street (Goldman Sachs, Morgan Stanley, Merrill Lynch, Lehman Brothers, and Bear Stearns) still awarded over $65 billion in compensation and benefits to their employees. Yet they did not have sufficient coverage to protect Madoff investors? Were there other sources of funds aside from premiums paid in by SIPC's members?

From SIPC's 2008 annual report:

"The sources of money for the SIPC Fund are assessments collected from SIPC members and interest on investments in United States Government securities. As a supplement to the SIPC Fund, a revolving line of credit was obtained from a consortium of banks. In addition, if the need arises, the SEC has the authority to lend SIPC up to $1 billion, which it, in turn, would borrow from the United States Treasury."[8]

At the end of 2008, just prior to the onslaught of billions of dollars in requests for restitution from Madoff investors, the SIPC Fund had approximately $1.7 billion. As to the insurance premiums collected, or as SIPC liked to define them, the member assessments, "for calendar year 2008 and through March 31, 2009, each member's assessment was $150."[9]

Could that be a misprint in SIPC's annual report? Is it possible that an entity such as SIPC would collect an annual premium of only $150 from its members? In fact, it was not only possible—it was reality. Merrill Lynch, Goldman Sachs, Morgan Stanley, Lehman Brothers, J.P. Morgan, and every other broker-dealer was paying a mere $150 annual premium into the SIPC fund for the benefit of being able to imprint that SIPC stamp of protection on their brokerage statements and inform their clients that they were properly covered. Could this token premium have been strictly a one-time event over the course of SIPC's history? Anything but. Member assessments were a mere $150 annually per member from 1996 through 2008.[10]

Of all the injustices and abusive behaviors suffered by investors during the market meltdown and subsequent economic crisis, this was an especially heinous travesty. Individuals purchasing insurance for homes, health, autos, or disability pay thousands of dollars for such coverage. Small businesses pay many thousands of dollars in annual premiums for product liability. Doctors pay tens of thousands of dollars for malpractice insurance. Yet an industry that had just prevailed upon the federal government to relax its capital ratios so it could double and triple its risk paid an annual assessment of $150 per member into its insurance fund for the benefit of investors? What does that tell you about how Wall Street management viewed the safety and protection of its customers? How much did each of these firms pay for the weekly floral arrangements in their executive offices? How much did each of these firms pay to shuttle their executives around in private car services? A lot more than $150.

Where were the SEC and the General Accounting Office to whom SIPC reported, during those years when Wall Street was paying $150 in annual assessments? In fact, the GAO had raised warning signals about the SIPC Fund in April 2003: "The SIPC Fund was at risk in the case of failure of one or more of the large securities firms. SEC found that even if SIPC were to triple the fund in size, a very large liquidation could deplete the fund. Therefore, SEC suggested that SIPC examine alternative strategies for dealing with the costs of such a large liquidation. SIPC management agreed to bring this issue to the attention of the Board of Directors, who evaluates the adequacy of the fund on a regular basis."[11] The fact that the members continued to pay $150 premiums for the next five years after that report tells us all we need to know about how the directors viewed the GAO's recommendation.

Of course, most investors—and Madoff investors specifically—probably didn't know at that point that selected individuals on

SIPC's board worked at the Federal Reserve, the US Treasury, Charles Schwab and Company, and SIPC itself. Simply one more indication of the incestuous nature of the entire dynamic masquerading as investor protection.

In a complaint filed in 2010 in United States District Court in New Jersey, on behalf of Madoff investors against the president and directors of SIPC, Chaitman highlighted the following SIPC shortcomings from the aforementioned 2003 GAO review that had been identified by the SEC:

- Some statements in SIPC's brochure and Web site might overstate the extent of SIPC coverage and mislead investors.
- There was insufficient guidance for SIPC personnel and trustees to follow when determining whether claimants have established valid unauthorized trading claims, one principle source of investor complaints.
- SIPC lacks a retention policy for records generated in liquidations where SIPC appoints an outside trustee.
- The SIPC fund was at risk in the case of failure of one or more of the large securities firms.
- SIPC had inadequate controls over the fees awarded to trustees and their counsel for services rendered and their expenses.[12]

The final point recently garnered new relevance when it was revealed that the Madoff trustee, Irving Picard, and staff had accrued fees in excess of $700 million by mid-2013.

In light of these findings, published by the SEC in its 2003 report, it is inexcusable that SIPC and its Wall Street member firms left the annual assessments at $150 for the next five years—a period during which Wall Street firms dramatically increased their leverage and accompanying risk.

Madoff investors were led to believe that SIPC coverage would be in place for all investors based upon an exchange in a December 2009 congressional hearing on SIPC reform, chaired by Representative Paul Kanjorski (D-PA).[13] That coverage of up to a $500,000 per-customer limit, based upon the final Madoff brokerage statement, would have gone a long way to helping many innocent—and now destitute—investors get back on their feet. But shortly thereafter, SIPC appointed a trustee and decided to pursue a different track of restitution based upon net winners versus net losers in the scam. The legal battles that ensued introduced terms such as "net equity," "clawbacks," and "legitimate expectations" into the financial pages of our major business periodicals. Lost in the midst of the legal challenges and salacious headlines in the Madoff scam was the pain and anguish of so many ordinary American citizens. Here's what the founder of the Bernard Madoff Victims Coalition shared with me:

> I feel the sincerity in your email. Thank you. It's been a tough struggle for the last 8 months. I don't think anyone, no matter how empathetic, can fully understand what it means to have everything you ever worked for taken away in the blink of an eye. Initially, we reeled from the loss of money, but as time goes on we realize that it wasn't just a financial loss. Many victims feel betrayed by our country, unprotected by the alleged laws that are in place, and helpless because of those in charge of executing the laws. That's a huge loss. Then there's the loss of homes, medical care, legacies to children and grandchildren. The list of horrors goes on and on.
>
> There are so many aspects of our battles. We have the failure of the SEC to find the fraud. Then we have their failure to

recognize it when Harry Markopolos handed them the facts. They even missed warnings from their own internal counsel. This must be addressed so that no one else will ever have to experience the devastation we are feeling.

Another aspect, and one I think is more applicable now is the fact that one man (Irving Picard) has unilaterally opted to change the SIPC protection by arbitrarily changing the basis for payment of claims. I've researched past SIPC cases, and am in contact with my counterpart in the Stanford case and see the SIPC pattern— their rules are so vague (intentionally?) that they can be interpreted any way that suits SIPC's needs. This is also a complaint issued by the GAO in a report they issued. Picard is literally robbing people of money they are owed. The travesty continues with the fact that the SEC has oversight over SIPC and is standing by and letting this happen. Where is the justice? Where is the trust? How can an investor have confidence?

The SEC failed, SIPC is lying and the law is in place. So, if I remember my high school civics' lesson, it is the responsibility of congress to ensure the laws that are in place are enforced properly. As a group, we have contacted every congressman and senator and explained our situation (regarding net equity and IRS payment of taxes on phantom income) and asked for help. We did our homework and have secured the name of every chief of staff, counsel and/or legislative aid in each office. We have a committee calling the offices asking for support. To date, we only have a handful.

I don't get it.

These are stories that need to be told so that the entire Investment community knows the facts. We need restitution. We deserve recovery. We did nothing wrong and yet we are being forced into fighting to defend ourselves. This is America—how can this happen?

It's been my feelings that this information must be shared so others can learn and be forewarned. I look forward to pursuing any avenues that might help.

Thanks,

Ronnie Sue Ambrosino, Coordinator,

Bernard Madoff Victims Coalition[14]

Ambrosino and other coalition members fought for what they believed in, and what had been represented to them by the SEC and SIPC over a period of years. There was precedent, detailed in a financial fraud case involving *New Times Securities,* for SIPC compensating innocent investors who had accrued fictitious, reinvested profits from a Ponzi scam.[15] In the aforementioned December 2009 hearing, Kanjorski questioned the head of SIPC, Stephen Harbeck, as to why SIPC would not simply go back and reassess its Wall Street members for the funds to compensate the Madoff victims. Despite these preconceived beliefs and questions, the trustee appointed by SIPC, Irving Picard, plowed ahead in pursuit of the net winners on behalf of the net losers.

In her testimony to Congress, Helen Davis Chaitman described the true motivation behind this unorthodox approach:

There is only one reason why SIPC has violated the clear mandates of SIPA. SIPC's and Picard's conduct saves Wall Street about $1.5 billion in SIPC insurance . . . Congress pointed out to SIPC that its failure to appropriately assess the Wall Street firms for SIPC insurance left SIPC incapable of handling a major liquidation. Despite warnings from the GAO and from the House Financial Services Committee, SIPC persisted during the entire period from 1996–2008 to charge a mere $150 per year to each firm for hundreds of billions of dollars of SIPC insurance. Thus,

Goldman Sachs paid $150 per year for the privilege of printing on tens of billions of dollars of trade confirmations that the customers' accounts were insured up to $500,000 by SIPC.[16]

The simple fact is that customers of all brokerage houses in our nation were and still are at much greater risk than they could have ever imagined. How does any entity—let alone an entire industry—allow member firms to pay only $150 in annual premiums for an insurance fund? In order to replenish its fund, SIPC is now, much as in its formative years, assessing member firms a premium based on a percentage of the firm's net operating revenue. Playing catch up, however, is of little help to countless Madoff investors left unprotected by regulators and SIPC.

Does a $150 annual premium from SIPC member firms for 13 years border on corruption? A disheartened Madoff victim expressed the sense of despair and disenfranchisement shared by so many in our nation:

It's become painfully clear that *nothing* happens to the big guys as long as they are making campaign contributions. Corzine at MF Global . . . off the hook ($1.2 billion), J.P. Morgan . . . off the hook. Barclays . . . off the hook. In the case of Madoff, all the insiders, Picower, J.P. Morgan, Shana Madoff, the kids, et al., off the hook.

The SEC goes as far as to admit that they are virtually powerless against the big boys. It seems that the only people that are ever held accountable are the *victims* of the wrongdoing by the big guys that are stealing their money.

I believe that this country has hit the tipping point where big money buys the legalized victimization of the general population, those naive enough to place their trust in the system.

As a Madoff victim, I have a front row seat to the levels of corruption in government. It goes from the very bottom (local zoning boards) to the very top (the Supreme Court). The corruption isn't always quid pro quo (at the highest level anyway), it is often the acquiescence to the most expeditious, politically non-interruptive end. An example is the way the Supreme Court refused to hear the appeal on the definition of "net equity."

With the appeal left in place, a customer of a SIPC-member, SEC-approved broker does not know if there is insurance until *after* the crime has occurred and the attorney for the insurance company decides whether the insurance company wants to pay it or not. Do insurance companies *ever* want to pay?

. . . I don't know where we have any room to talk about justice.[17]

Let this be the legacy of the management on Wall Street and their bedmates, the regulators and legislators in Washington—on both sides of the aisle. They have presided over the destruction of any sense of fair play and trust in the American financial system.

NINE
CODE OF SILENCE

The only way to deal with a whistleblower's accusations—again, every single time and again often against your own instincts—is with a hyper-bias toward believing that the informant is onto something big. Such a bias must impel you to investigate every claim ferociously.

—Jack and Susy Welch, Reuters, May 1, 2012

FROM THE OUTSIDE, WALL STREET APPEARS TO BE IN-volved in many different businesses. From consumer banking to investment banking, from trading and sales to mergers and acquisitions, from venture capital to private equity, from research to prime brokerage, Wall Street represents a diverse line of businesses offering a wide array of products.

From the inside, though, Wall Street is really only engaged in one business. Its single product has varying degrees of value depending on the specific situation. Often it is deemed virtually priceless and market participants will go to incredible lengths to gain access to it. All of the aforementioned lines of business on Wall Street ultimately come under the purview of this overarching pursuit. Of course, I'm talking about the information business. Those working on Wall Street know that information is everything.

No matter what discipline you're in, the one with the most information holds all the cards. Information moves markets and changes valuations on a broad level, as well as within specific market sectors and individual securities. Information provides the edge that is often the difference between winning and losing on Wall Street, and those with access to it can often grow what might otherwise be a run-of-the-mill business into a veritable franchise. All this said, managing the flow of information so that markets remain fair, free, and balanced presents enormous challenges.

Within firms, managers are charged with ensuring that the exchange of information and subsequent transactions conform to the rules of the industry. Aside from the managers within a specific business, there are also typically independent risk managers to further review positions and exposures. Additionally, compliance professionals are charged with overseeing an array of businesses so that regulations are not violated. And finally, outside of the firms, regulators from an array of agencies, both governmental and non-governmental, are challenged to maintain order and decorum across the entire industry.

Invariably there will be reckless drivers and others engaging in dangerous and perhaps illegal maneuvers while negotiating the twists and turns of Wall Street. This is true in every industry. Those who call attention to such violations, we call whistleblowers.

A whistleblower, under most legal definitions, is an employee who uncovers evidence of corruption or wrongdoing at his/her workplace and makes the difficult decision to disclose that information to the media, organizational executives, lawmakers, or other government authorities.

One would think whistleblowers and whistleblowing would be welcomed by executives in government, at regulatory organizations, and in private enterprise. But not always. Some view it as a threat or a challenge to an otherwise welcomed status quo. To this end, there are not-for-profit organizations such as the Government Accountability Project (GAP) and the Project on Government Oversight (POGO) that work with whistleblowers to promote corporate and government accountability.

As reported by GAP, since the year 2000 whistleblowers from all walks of life have exposed: medications responsible for the deaths of tens of thousands; White House officials' wrongful tampering with climate science data; defective HIV-testing kits being issued to Indian hospitals (showing AIDS-tainted blood as being "OK" to distribute); dog-killing pet medications; unsafe food production practices at a peanut butter plant, which led to multiple deaths; grossly unsafe practices at a nuclear facility in Washington state; and multiple problems at the SEC, including hedge fund oversight corruption and overall incompetence in heeding whistleblowers[1]

Certainly we've witnessed sufficient evidence to question the competency of regulators at the SEC. Corruption, though, is a different matter, and one that puts the question of integrity within our government front and center, not only for investors but for the public at large.

Whistleblower extraordinaire Harry Markopolos certainly went unheeded by the SEC despite having provided 29 red flags to the SEC regarding the scam perpetrated by Bernie Madoff. Markopolos has since been hailed as a hero, but if we were to listen strictly to the SEC's internal review after the Madoff scam unfolded, we would have learned little about their shortcomings in promoting and protecting whistleblowers. In fact, the SEC had a whistleblower bounty program in place while Madoff was orchestrating his scam, yet the whistles on Wall Street were largely silent.

Are we to think that Wall Street was uniquely well behaved while the SEC whistleblower program was in place? Or were the

SEC and Wall Street jointly more interested in promoting a code of silence than an air of transparency during these years? POGO shed light on this dark and quiet corner of the SEC: "For more than 20 years, the Securities and Exchange Commission (SEC) has had a program in place to reward whistleblowers who provide the agency with information about insider trading. But a new audit by the SEC Office of Inspector General (OIG) reveals that the program has almost never been used, is barely recognized inside or outside the SEC, and has fundamental design flaws. It turns out the SEC has received very few applications in the past two decades for bounties under the program—and only five people have actually received payments since the program first began."[2]

FIGURE 2.   SEC WHISTLEBLOWER AWARDS

YEAR	WHISTLEBLOWER	AWARD
1989	Whistleblower #1	$3,500
2001	Whistleblower #2	$18,152
2002	Whistleblower #3	$29,079
2005	Whistleblower #4	$17,500
2006	Whistleblower #4	$29,920
2007	Whistleblower #5	$6,166
2009	Whistleblower #4	$55,220

Credit: Author created with data culled from the Project on Government Oversight's "Not Much Bounty for SEC Whistleblower Program," April 5, 2010, http://pogoblog.typepad .com/pogo/2010/04/if-the-sec-has-a-whistleblower-program-but-nobody-ever-uses-it -does-it-really-exist.html.

In assessing the component parts of 20 years, five recipients of whistleblower payments, and total bounties of less than $160,000, all we can conclude is that this program was little more than a charade. Investors would probably prefer to think that no whistleblower program existed at all than one that was so ineffectual.

POGO goes on to highlight that the SEC's Office of Inspector General found six major faults in the program, including:

1. Limited recognition of the program both by the public and within the SEC.

2. Standards by which bounty applications were measured were not well defined.

3. Weak internal policies at the SEC for directing staff in assessing bounty applications.

4. Whistleblowers were typically not apprised of the status of their applications.

5. A lack of systems to monitor the timely processing of applications.

6. The certifications connected with bounty referrals were often incomplete.[3]

Is the American public supposed to believe that the SEC had good intentions with this program, but was simply weak in terms of execution? If any government agency was in need of a robust whistleblower program, it was the SEC. This data is simply further evidence of how the SEC failed both in form and function to protect investors and the public at large.

A few short years after the release of the POGO report, the US attorney for the southern district of New York, Preet Bharara, commented that insider trading on Wall Street was "rampant and routine and that this criminal behavior was known, encouraged and exploited by authority figures in several investment funds."[4]

Few individuals would have a better vantage point than the prosecutor who might ultimately bring charges against those engaged in insider trading and other market transgressions. Bharara's comment supports the claim that 20 years of the code of silence on Wall Street has welcomed a criminal element into our markets. And it's never been easier, with the lax regulatory culture that has permeated the SEC and the financial regulatory system at large.

If Harry Markopolos's unsuccessful attempt to blow the whistle on Bernie Madoff tells us anything, it's that other financial frauds could have been either mitigated or averted if other whistleblowers had stepped forward, or not been ignored by those in power when they did. While Markopolos gained national notoriety given the level of his persistence in pursuing Madoff, America was never fully introduced to Leyla Wydler, Eileen Foster, and Peter Scannell.

LEYLA WYDLER

Leyla Wydler claims she was fired by Stanford Financial in late 2002 because of her unwillingness to sell the certificates of deposits central to Allen Stanford's Ponzi operation, which was centered within his bank on Antigua while also very much utilizing his Texas-based broker-dealer to attract funds to grow the enterprise. Stanford's operation afforded him a lavish lifestyle replete with the trappings of high society. It also caused Wydler to take a harder look at what was really transpiring within Stanford Financial. After being fired and in the midst of her pursuit of retribution via arbitration, Wydler contacted the SEC in late 2004 to lay out all the red flags in her counterclaim against the company.[5]

As reported by *Forbes*, Wydler warned in her letter to the SEC that Stanford Financial was "the subject of a lingering corporate fraud scandal perpetrated as a massive Ponzi scheme that will destroy the life savings of many, damage the reputation of all associated parties, ridicule securities and banking authorities, and shame the United States of America."[6] Wydler delivered her letter to the NASD and major periodicals including the *Wall Street Journal* and *Washington Post*. Shortly thereafter Stanford Financial decided not to continue to fight Wydler's case and pursued a settlement. A full four years later and with significantly greater losses involved, Wydler's projections came true.

EILEEN FOSTER

A senior executive at Countrywide Mortgage named Eileen Foster was also rebuffed in her attempt to shed light on pervasive fraud within that organization. Foster unearthed evidence of systemic fraud within Countrywide's mortgage origination pipeline. The fraud ranged from improperly inputting personal financial data to forging mortgage documents and almost everything in between so as to facilitate the funding of mortgages that were quickly securitized and then sold. Her attempts to raise this problem to the attention of senior executives within Countrywide were ignored. Shortly after Countrywide's takeover by Bank of America, Foster was asked to speak with government regulators regarding the reports of fraud. Foster was fired shortly before that meeting took place. In an interview with *60 Minutes*, Foster shares her belief that she was fired after informing an individual within the firm that she planned on being forthright with the regulators:

> STEVE KROFT: Do you believe that there are people at Countrywide who belong behind bars?
>
> EILEEN FOSTER: Yes.
>
> KROFT: Do you want to give me their names?
>
> FOSTER: No.
>
> KROFT: Would you give their names to a grand jury if you were asked?
>
> FOSTER: Yes. . . .
>
> KROFT: Did you have any discussions with anybody at Countrywide or Bank of America about what you should say to the federal regulators when they came?
>
> FOSTER: I got a call from an individual who, you know, suggested how—how I should handle the questions that would

be coming from the regulators, made some suggestions that
downplayed the severity of the situation.

KROFT: They wanted you to spin it and you said you wouldn't?

FOSTER: Uh-huh (affirm).

KROFT: And the next day you were terminated?

FOSTER: Uh-huh (affirm).

KROFT: I mean, it seems like somebody at Countrywide or Bank
of America did not want you to talk to federal regulators.

FOSTER: No, that was part of it, no, they absolutely did not.[7]

One might think that Foster would have been the first person
called by President Barack Obama's task force to investigate mortgage fraud launched in late 2011. Given that whistleblowers like
Foster were not fully embraced, one can only wonder as to just how
committed the task force was to finding the total truth regarding
mortgage fraud in the Wall Street pipeline. In fact, in mid-2013
Bloomberg reported that this task force massively misrepresented its
data and findings from what can only be characterized as embar-
rassingly low levels.

PETER SCANNELL

Peter Scannell worked at Putnam Investments in the early 2000s.
While there he detected abusive trading practices, characterized as
market timing, ongoing within the firm's funds, by employees as
well as clients of the firm. He brought his knowledge of these practices initially to the attention of Putnam management and then to
the attention of the SEC's office in Boston (the same office that
Harry Markopolos tried to engage). Scannell was largely rebuffed
both by Putnam's management and the SEC, but his attempts to do
the right thing caught the attention of others.

Prior to fully blowing the whistle, Scannell suffered a true market related beating. He shared details of this vicious assault at a congressional hearing:

> Suddenly, without warning my car door was opened and I was being grabbed by my jacket and pulled out of the door, I still had my seatbelt on and struggled to face my attacker. As I looked up I could see a large burley man with a full beard, New York Yankee's cap and grey sweatshirt that had "Boilermakers Local 5" emblazoned across the chest area in large bold letters. This was happening in split seconds and I felt something smashing down on my head while he was strangely talking very loud but furious. He said I better "Shut the f—up" and repeated this and some reference to my working for Putnam a number of times while smashing my head and left hand, repeatedly with what the police told me later was a brick. . . . Blood was spattered against the inside of my driver's door and there was a big gash in the car's upholstery. I was shaking uncontrollably. Evidently I had been hanging out of my driver's side door held up by my seatbelt for almost an hour before help arrived. After this horrific attack I am suffering with disturbing neurological problems including headaches, confusion, dizziness as well as deeply disturbing emotional trauma.[8]

The intimidation and suffering Scannell experienced did not deter him from providing a wealth of details and discoveries to the federal regulators. But it wasn't until he brought the information to state authorities in Massachusetts that some degree of movement took place: "One of the most disturbing matters for me still remains, and that is the treatment I received from the very Commission that should have been honoring my efforts . . . They had refused to look at the 'can of worms' I had delivered to their door."[9]

Scannell's case is particularly disturbing. Ignoring whistle-blowers is a practice too often tolerated by regulators and financial management. Intimidating whistleblowers is a practice too often connected with organized crime. It's not a big leap, then, to wonder whether financial management allowed—or at least ignored—certain criminal elements at work within its sphere.

Putnam did ultimately settle the charges of market timing, but more as a result of the initial pressure applied and efforts undertaken by the Massachusetts secretary of state, not by the SEC. Senior individuals within both Putnam and the SEC, whom Scannell believes stymied his efforts to reveal the abusive trading practices, went through the revolving door and on with their careers.

The cases highlighted by Markopolos, Wydler, Foster, Scannell, and other whistleblowers suggest pervasive and corrosive corruption within our markets. Increasingly investors, consumers, and the general public are recognizing that the information superhighway on Wall Street operates with widely divergent rules of the road. The Wall Street police appear increasingly unable or unwilling to uphold their mandate to protect investors. The cries for meaningful justice rather than mere fines fell largely upon the deaf ears of regulators and government attorneys who, post-crash, are trying to portray themselves as rigorous and respectable after years of egregious failures that culminated in the market meltdown and economic crisis.

Against this backdrop David Einhorn, a high-profile investment manager, voiced the distrust felt by so many, writing about the lax regulatory oversight of Allied Capital:

> I care that the SEC and other regulators seem to have stopped enforcing laws against corporate malfeasance. I care that company officials can lie with impunity on public conference calls. And I have been appalled that the government officials overseeing

the lending programs that Allied has defrauded are so indifferent and unwilling to act even when presented with clear evidence of abuse. The overall lack of law enforcement is startling. If we are going to permit the retribution against the whistleblowers shown in this story—defamation, investigation, invasion of privacy and so forth—then we surrender public free speech. If we allow the people in this story to operate outside the law, then we nourish a corrupt business culture. Rather than turn a blind eye to the fraud I witnessed, I made a decision to stand up and speak out despite the consequences. I hope my story inspires regulators and government agencies to do the right thing.[10]

The aforementioned whistleblowers were all on the outside looking into the opacity that permeated our financial regulators. To gain a real appreciation of the ineptitude masquerading as financial regulation, we need to gain an insider's perspective. Let's meet Joe Sciddurlo, Peter Sivere, and Gary Aguirre.

JOE SCIDDURLO

In late 2010, a full two years after the demise of Lehman Brothers, a regulatory coordinator at FINRA named Joe Sciddurlo made a recommendation to the regulator's executives as to how they could more aggressively monitor the annual audit worksheet of the banks and brokers overseen by this self-regulatory organization. Sciddurlo was not a naive young professional trying to create a project to impress, but rather a veteran of 20-plus years in the industry with the bulk of that time spent as a forensic accountant in the corporate and investment bank at Citigroup.

Sciddurlo was specifically targeting the manner in which Oppenheimer & Company was accounting for its auction-rate securities

(ARS) obligations. According to Sciddurlo, the company carried these ARS obligations on the books of the firm's holding company instead of as a liability by the broker-dealer. That bit of financial artifice struck this regulator as a blatant violation of generally accepted accounting principles.

Sciddurlo sent an e-mail to his superiors, writing that "a 'quality of earnings' check coupled with an inquisitive RC [regulatory coordination] should prevent a reoccurrence of Lehman as the tough questions emanating from this process should dissuade the member firm from employing aggressive accounting techniques."[11] His e-mail was met with a tersely worded but dismissive rejoinder, a subsequent warning regarding his performance, and ultimately a dismissal five months later.

In reply to a question regarding his firing, Sciddurlo boldly stated, "I was trouble. I was ethical and competent . . . I agree with Madoff whistle blower Harry Markopolos' claim that Finra is corrupt and incompetent (and) in cahoots with the large broker-dealers at the expense of the investing public."[12]

In a statement that is emblematic of the allegations launched by Lieutenant Colonel Elton Johnson in the *Amerivet v. FINRA* case, "Sciddurlo said he doesn't remember any direct order to go after small firms harder than big ones while working at Finra. But, he said, that was the 'mindset.' 'They (screw) the small firms. They don't give a (crap) about the small firms. What pays their salaries? It's the big firms,' he said."[13]

While there is little public evidence to date supporting or negating the dismissal of Sciddurlo from FINRA, the points he raised were fully consistent with a mandate to protect investors. To dismiss rather than embrace an individual who would raise such issues certainly calls into question how strongly FINRA holds true to its mission to protect investors.

PETER SIVERE

As in Peter Scannell's story, other firms were also entangled in the practice of market timing, also known as after-hours trading. In short, this illegal activity encompassed the trading of mutual fund shares after the market had closed, and thus at the closing price of the day, but subsequent to market moving news having been released which, invariably, would have an impact on the value of the fund. In essence, this after-hours trading allowed those engaged in the practice to effectively steal value—that is, money—from all the other shareholders in that fund.

This trading was often undertaken by hedge funds that executed the trades through the banks' trading desks. In addition to executing the trade, banks and brokers often provided lines of credit with attractive fee arrangements, allowing hedge funds to engage in this illicit practice with borrowed funds.

Into this web stepped a relatively young compliance professional named Peter Sivere at J.P. Morgan. Sivere worked on a team that was tasked with providing documentation to the SEC for an investigation into after-hours trading. In the course of his job, Sivere unearthed what he believed to be incriminating evidence and presented it to his superiors to submit to the SEC. Six months later Sivere inquired as to what had happened to the documents that were supposed to have been presented to the commission.

Within a matter of weeks, Sivere was presented with a termination agreement—which he did not accept—for insubordination. He immediately contacted internal audit at J.P. Morgan to report that he believed he was being retaliated against for questioning compliance management on this issue. He then contacted the SEC on his own to provide the regulator with documentation of the illegal activity and inquired about a potential bounty for doing so. When informed that he was not eligible for such a reward, he provided the information regardless.[14]

Sivere was cleared of any wrongdoing by J.P. Morgan's internal audit unit but was demoted by the firm upon his return from a paid leave of absence. He was subsequently dismissed from the firm.

Sivere contacted the Occupational Safety & Health Administration (OSHA), the SEC, the NASD, and NYSE regarding his case. OSHA issued a preliminary finding that J.P. Morgan had retaliated against Sivere and ordered his reinstatement. In response, lawyers for J.P. Morgan wrote to OSHA, arguing that Sivere could not have been a whistleblower, in part because he had "sought payment from the SEC."[15] The letter noted that the SEC had "encouraged" J.P. Morgan to provide this information.[16] Concerned that this had damaged his case, Sivere dropped his complaint and negotiated a settlement with J.P. Morgan.[17] Subsequently, an internal probe led by the SEC's inspector general determined that an SEC lawyer with whom Sivere had communicated had violated both Sivere's confidentiality and the rules of the SEC in the process.[18] The SEC's IG referred this lawyer for possible disciplinary action but none was forthcoming. It was subsequently reported that the SEC lawyer who "had ratted out Sivere" was George Demos.[19] The lawyer quietly resigned from the SEC and ultimately but unsuccessfully pursued public office.[20]

Additional attempts by Sivere to have his case heard by legal review boards and judicial bodies were largely unsuccessful. He filed an ethics complaint against Demos with the Disciplinary Committee of the First Appellate Division of the New York State Supreme Court, and the proceeding was ultimately dismissed, with a determination that there was an insufficient basis for finding professional misconduct by the lawyer.[21] During these procedures, Demos argued that even if he—or someone else in the SEC—had disclosed this information, it would have had no bearing on the disciplinary proceedings because Sivere had never been a client of either him or the SEC.[22] This argument was apparently successful, notwithstanding the conclusion of the IG that Demos had violated Sivere's confidentiality and the SEC rules.

As for J.P. Morgan and its engagement with the now-defunct hedge fund in question, Canary Capital, no charges were ever filed against the bank despite the fact that several other major institutions later reached settlements as a result of similar SEC inquiries. While J.P. Morgan went about its business and Demos moved on to the next stage of his career, Sivere suffered immeasurable emotional and professional pain. In an attempt to redress this travesty, Sivere has been anything but silent in trying to shed light on what transpired in his case. Not many individuals have the courage to continue looking for justice after such a heinous violation. While the financial industry is wont to present an air of meaningful integrity within its compliance oversight, Sivere paints a distinctly different picture of what he experienced within J.P. Morgan. "I raised a lot of issues that I think they didn't want to know because they had to deal with it either in a compliance or legal way, and it brought up a lot of issues . . . that I think upper management sometimes would rather not deal with . . . I think they [would] rather have somebody just click on something and say they reviewed it and give those stats to the regulator without really having any substance in the review or a basis of why you're doing a review."[23]

Sivere continues to make his case about the problems within the world of compliance on Wall Street. In our e-mail exchange, he summed it up this way: "My experience is that almost everyone on the inside of these banking conglomerates are sheep. If you make big money for the bank you can do no wrong. Management in most cases would rather pay a fine than deal with the systemic issues and culture within the organization. Jail is the only moral compass that will change this mind set."

GARY AGUIRRE

Up until now, the whistleblower cases highlight the unsuccessful and ineffective manner in which our financial regulators have addressed—or perhaps I should say, not addressed—Ponzi schemes, mortgage fraud, after-hours trading, and shady accounting. The costs connected to the regulatory failures of these cases and so many more are virtually incalculable. The costs are not only monetary, but social: a loss of trust and confidence in the markets and our system of capitalism.

If ever there were an individual that investors and our nation should hold up as a hero for exposing our failed financial regulatory system and the corrupt crony capitalism that has developed between Wall Street and Washington, it is Gary Aguirre. This former senior counsel for the SEC is tireless in his pursuit of justice within the corporate, financial, and regulatory arenas. He was certainly prescient in testimony before the Senate Judiciary Committee in 2006 and an industry conference in 2007 when he compared the market environment fostered by lax SEC enforcement to those conditions that delivered the crash of 1929. These conditions centered on systemic market abuses and excessive leverage within the large Wall Street firms. True to form, neither the SEC nor any other regulatory agencies showed any interest in embracing Aguirre or lending credence to his forewarning.[24]

Aguirre specifically focused on that "rampant and routine" insider trading. The case made by this courageous and heroic legal hawk against a hedge fund titan lays out in spades how truly corrupt are the large moneyed interests within Wall Street management and how deeply embedded they are with their political and regulatory friends in Washington.

Aguirre had a promising career developing at the SEC. He received a two-step pay raise at the end of his first year for "consistently going the extra mile, and then some."[25] He then touched the third rail upon which the corrupt current between Washington and Wall Street traveled "while leading an investigation of suspected insider trading by Pequot Capital Management, the largest hedge fund in the world at that time."[26] Shortly thereafter Aguirre was pushed out the door of the SEC. More often than not, a dismissal of the sort that Aguirre experienced would have been the end of the case. But Aguirre was determined to see the truth win out.

A Senate committee opened an investigation in early 2006 to assess the merits of Aguirre's dismissal from the SEC, which contested Aguirre's allegation that his supervisors had provided preferential treatment to a high-profile and powerful Wall Street executive. After almost two years of review, the Senate Finance and Judiciary Committee vindicated Aguirre and issued a 108-page report validating his case.

The core of Aguirre's case against Pequot centered on the fact that Art Samberg, the hedge fund titan who had created Pequot in 1999, allegedly received inside information about General Electric Capital Corporation's takeover of Heller Financial to generate an $18 million profit.[27] Additionally, Aguirre addresses that Samberg allegedly benefited from inside information on Microsoft to generate $14.7 million in illicit profits.[28] Aguirre maintained that Samberg had engaged and ultimately hired a Microsoft employee, David Zilkha, who provided this proprietary information to Samberg.

In the process of making the case against Samberg and Pequot, the evidentiary trail from the GE Capital takeover of Heller led to John Mack, who was the incoming CEO of Morgan Stanley and one of the most powerful men on Wall Street. Aguirre moved to subpoena Mack. At this point, the praise from within the SEC that had been regularly directed Aguirre's way ceased. The SEC's enforcement division created an obstacle course for Aguirre, and his supervisors blocked the subpoena, telling him that Mack had "juice" and "political clout."[29]

The Government Accountability Project brought badly needed transparency to this intrigue by highlighting "why the Mack subpoena was essential and expressed concern that 'treating Mack differently is [not] consistent with the Commission's mission.'"[30] The Senate Report tells what happened next: "'Just days after Aguirre sent an e-mail to Associate Director Paul Berger detailing his allegations, his supervisors prepared a negative re-evaluation outside the SEC's ordinary performance appraisal process.' One month later, the SEC fired him without warning."[31]

"The Pequot investigation appeared to have run its course when the SEC released its "Case Closing Report" in December 2006, explaining its decision to close the entire investigation, including Pequot's trading in Microsoft options, without filing charges."[32] One can only assume that Samberg and his colleagues at Pequot breathed a sigh of relief at that development.[33]

Most attorneys would have recognized at this point that one does not take on the powerful elite on Wall Street while trying to make an insider trading case. Aguirre is not like most attorneys. Being fired by the SEC merely stoked his fire to scale the Wall Street–Washington fortress and make the case. Having initially undertaken this case as SEC counsel, Aguirre, now as a private citizen, continued over the next four years to doggedly pursue those involved in this case.

Utilizing court orders and, ultimately, the Freedom of Information Act, Aguirre was able to gain access to SEC documents pertaining to its Pequot investigation. Having gone to great lengths already to derail Aguirre, the SEC maintained its obstructive manner and objected to providing this information. Despite those hurdles, Aguirre continued to piece together the evidence and make his case, which he delivered to SEC chairman Chris Cox in early 2009.[34] But still the SEC continued to resist in filing a formal case against Samberg and Pequot.[35] Another year passed. Lesser men may have wilted, but the passage of time only served to further steel Aguirre's resolve.

On May 26, 2010, Aguirre made a motion against the SEC to gain access to more Pequot records, and keep the pressure on in the process. He maintained he was entitled to the records under FOIA, given that the commission had not filed a case against Pequot, Samberg, or related parties. The SEC filed charges the very next day.[36]

That same day, six years after Aguirre first launched the investigation, Pequot Capital Management and the hedge fund firm's founder, Arthur Samberg, agreed to a $28 million settlement for having illegally sourced and utilized information provided to him. Samberg had already announced that he was shutting down his hedge fund; as part of this settlement, he agreed to be barred from working as an investment adviser.[37]

Clearly Aguirre had displayed Herculean fortitude in his pursuit of justice and ultimate victory in this battle with Samberg, Pequot, and the SEC. Aguirre had won a battle, but America was clearly losing the war from within. Recall that during this same time frame the US attorney for the southern district of New York had described insider trading on Wall Street as "rampant and routine."

In his letter to then-SEC chair Chris Cox, Aguirre details what he felt led to the failure of the SEC regarding the Pequot case: "It is difficult to overstate the extent to which Enforcement staff dropped the ball on its Pequot investigation, including the aspect dealing with Pequot's trading in Microsoft securities. It raises an obvious question: was Enforcement really trying? The report by two Senate committees implies it was not. It sure looks that way. . . .

"In short, the SEC dropped the most promising aspect of Pequot's trading in Microsoft options without conducting any real investigation. . . . It would not have been hard to find the crucial evidence needed to make the case."[38]

As for Aguirre, having worked tirelessly for six years, including four as a private individual, to make this case, he brought a wrongful termination suit against the SEC. Having vanquished Samberg and Pequot, Aguirre gained further vindication when the SEC agreed to pay him $755,000 to settle his wrongful termination claim. Aguirre had this to say about the investigation, "It's a shame the team I worked with at the SEC did not get to complete the Pequot investigation. The filing of the case in 2005 or 2006, *before the financial crisis,* would have been exactly what Wall Street elite needed to hear at the perfect moment: the SEC goes after big fish too."[39]

How many big fish got away up to that point and since then? We will never fully know.

And who intervened for John Mack and Morgan Stanley with the SEC powers that be when the SEC investigation first began? According to reports, it was Mary Jo White, a well-respected former prosecutor in the southern district of New York.[40] In true revolving door fashion, White went from a position as a prosecutor to one as a high-profile defense attorney at Debevoise & Plimpton representing powerful corporations and banks, including Morgan Stanley (which, at a time Mack was being considered for the position of CEO, had retained White to assess Mack's exposure to allegations of insider trading). In early 2013, she was nominated and subsequently confirmed as the next chairman of the SEC. Little doubt White knows exactly how the games between Wall Street and Washington are played. She has not been a spectator but rather a participant. Whether she will be as strong a chairman as she had been a prosecutor remains to be seen.

The Department of Justice did not pursue Samberg and Pequot criminally. They simply allowed the statute of limitations to expire prior to bringing a case. Aguirre explained to me in an e-mail exchange why Wall Street's big fish swim free:

> The SEC's conduct in protecting John Mack was not an isolated act of generosity. The SEC has made the top-level management of banks the nation's sacred cows.
>
> The most egregious example of the SEC's no prosecute policy for Wall Street management was its case against Rolf Breuer, former CEO of Deutsche Bank [for making a materially misleading statement regarding a potential acquisition]. The case was greenlighted all the way up to the desk of Enforcement Director Richard Walker. The file sat on his desk for three months when he recused himself. A few days later Walker's subordinate, Stephen Cutler, dumped the case.
>
> A couple months later Richard Walker would show up as a new general counsel for Deutsche Bank. This case offered a rare insight into how the SEC has a blind spot when it comes to prosecuting high-level Wall Street players. It only came to light because an SEC internal whistleblower, Darcy Flynn, had the courage to speak out.[41]

As for Stephen Cutler, he worked his way through the revolving door at the SEC and ultimately landed as the current general counsel at J.P. Morgan. The consequences of letting the big fish swim free are an overriding lack of trust and confidence in our markets, economy, regulators, and government. The costs associated with the breakdown of trust are incalculable.

In hindsight Aguirre leaves little to the imagination in excoriating the SEC's enforcement division while he was working on the Pequot case. He shared the following with me:

> By the time I was fired, I pretty much figured out what was going on at the SEC. I saw how the Enforcement Division—from the top down—had acted to block the Mack investigation, despite the fact that the evidentiary trail led directly to his door. I saw how SEC management would create a fictional rationale for not pursuing the investigation against John Mack, which would be immediately replaced with a new one as the last one imploded. Somewhere between the third and fourth fictionalized account, I understood just how deeply the corruption was embedded in Enforcement's management. By the time they fired me, my reaction was: Do they really think they'll get away with it?

Alleging corruption within SEC enforcement is a strong charge, but no single individual is more qualified to make it than Gary Aguirre. He then delivered the knockout:

> I do not believe the current leadership of the enforcement division wants the whistleblower program to become operative. The enforcement division leadership has a hostile attitude toward both internal and external whistleblowers. Contrary to the provisions of the Dodd-Frank Act, senior leadership at the enforcement division has done little to discourage enforcement staff from outing whistleblowers.[42]

Washington specifically and America at large could certainly benefit from having political leaders and regulatory officials displaying even a modicum of the character and courage displayed by Gary Aguirre.

The code of silence on Wall Street has buried an excruciating level of pain, loss, and anxiety for our entire nation. The individual stories of Harry Markopolos, Leyla Wydler, Eileen Foster, Peter Scannell, Joseph Sciddurlo, Peter Sivere, and Gary Aguirre are compelling. Each of these individuals held extraordinary evidence that would have been helpful in pursuing potential improprieties, if not outright and massive frauds. Yet each of them was ignored, intimidated, or fired.

TEN
POGO STICKS

The testimony had brought to light a shocking corruption in our banking system, a widespread repudiation of old-fashioned standards of honesty and fair dealing in the creation and sale of securities, and a merciless exploitation of the vicious possibilities of intricate corporate chicanery.

—Ferdinand Pecora, *Wall Street Under Oath*, 1939

AFTER EVERY GREAT NATIONAL CRISIS, WASHINGTON launches a commission to study the root causes of the disaster in the hope of learning why the tragic situation came to pass. Or at least to give the appearance of wanting to learn it.

In 1950, after decades of rampant organized crime, the federal government launched the United States Senate Special Committee to Investigate Crime in Interstate Commerce, the Kefauver Committee, with a special focus on how organized rackets had gained control of legal and illegal gambling and a strong foothold in political corruption. The President's Commission on the Assassination of President Kennedy, the Warren Commission, was launched to investigate the assassination of President John F. Kennedy. The Presidential Commission on the Space Shuttle Challenger Accident, also known as the Rogers Commission Report, reported to President Ronald Reagan that a faulty o-ring was responsible for the disintegration of the Challenger Shuttle 73 seconds into flight in June 1986. The 9/11 Commission was established to review how that fateful act of terrorism on US soil came to pass.

In order to learn the root causes of the market crash of 1929, the government enacted Senate Resolution 84 in early 1932 to look into the buying, selling, borrowing, and lending of stocks and securities. The initial work gained little momentum.

In early 1933, and only after 11 months of ineffectual investigation, Ferdinand Pecora took the reins as chief counsel to the United States Senate Committee on Banking and Currency. Pecora earned wide acclaim for his work in exposing the individuals, institutions, and practices that brought our country to its knees during the Great Depression. Pecora brought his New York, streetwise mentality and demeanor to bear upon financial executives all too used to the comforting confines of Wall Street's clubby executive suites. With unusually popular support reminiscent of a heavyweight champion, Pecora tirelessly tore down the longstanding facades of the nation's banking executives. The Pecora Investigation, as it came to be known, attained and maintains legendary status.

With no political agenda and a mission to pursue nothing but the truth, Pecora exemplified the Greatest Generation who came of age during the Depression and prioritized family, faith, and country over personal gain. With a clear disdain for the "banksters" whom he subpoenaed, Pecora's efforts drew daily coverage in the press. The public was consumed by his dogged pursuit of truth. The outrage and distrust coursing through the nation grew stronger as the commission's solicitation of support from the general public was met with endless stories of personal pain.

Pecora's first round of hearings included New York Stock Exchange president Richard Whitney and the chairman of National
City Bank, Charles Mitchell. This was not only the second-largest
bank in the country but, as the committee's report highlighted, was
also deemed to be a leader "in the orgy of speculation which led to
the business collapse."

> [Pecora] elicited confessions from Mitchell, for example, that se-
> verely damaged the chairman's reputation. Under Pecora's careful
> questioning, Mitchell confessed that his income in 1929, includ-
> ing bonuses and salary, totaled $1,206,195.02. He acknowledged
> selling National City stocks to a family member at a considerable
> loss in 1929 to avoid paying income taxes. Though Mitchell had
> not violated any laws, many judged his personal financial dealings
> as unethical. One editor expressed the sentiment of many when
> he asserted that "the only difference between a bank burglar and
> a bank president is that one works at night. . . ."
>
> Shortly after his appearance before the Senate Banking and
> Currency committee, Mitchell offered his resignation to the
> board of National City Bank. He left Washington a discredited
> man.[1]

The bankers found little sympathy among an increasingly im-
poverished public. Pecora's withering cross-examination of these
executives energized the American public. Washington was flooded
with calls praising Pecora's efforts and demanding further interrogation. As the fearless attorney exposed the shady dealings of the
banks and the bankers, Congress was simultaneously at work establishing a framework for meaningful regulatory oversight of the
financial system.

Prior to the final report by the Pecora Investigation in June 1934, Congress had implemented the Securities Act of 1933 and the Securities Exchange Act of 1934. These landmark pieces of legislation addressed the underwriting of new issue securities and established a formal regulator, the Securities Exchange Commission (SEC), to oversee a financial industry that had shown itself badly in need of policing. Beyond these two pieces of legislation, though, Congress also addressed the driving force behind the crash of 1929. They determined that what really precipitated the market crash and the resulting depression was the melding of commercial and investment banking practices.

The divorce papers separating commercial banking interests from investment banking were formally consummated in the Banking Act of 1933, which incorporated, and was often referred to as, the Glass-Steagall Act. Along with the separation of commercial and investment activities, the Banking Act of 1933 also was instrumental in the establishment of the Federal Deposit Insurance Commission (FDIC).[2]

There are many reasons so many economists have compared our current crisis to the Great Depression. In that light, Pecora and his investigative work cast a long shadow over President Barack Obama's announcement establishing the Financial Crisis Inquiry Commission (FCIC). The FCIC was also known as the Angelides Commission, after its chairman, Phil Angelides, a Democrat from California. The ten-member commission hoped to rise above the partisan fray and "examine the causes of the current financial and economic crisis in the United States."[3]

There were many similarities between the inputs of the investigative work undertaken by the Pecora Investigation and the FCIC. The FCIC also methodically reviewed millions of pages of documents, interviewed more than 700 witnesses, and held 19 days of public hearings in Washington, New York, and other communities badly impacted by the crisis. They also studied volumes of evidence and work produced both inside and outside of Washington.

But could the commission drill deeply enough to reveal the people and the practices that had caused our crisis? Would the bright lights of interrogation cause any of Wall Street's financial titans to wilt under pressure? Certainly the Angelides Commission must have been aware of being compared to the Pecora Investigation.

In an attempt to build popular support, the Angelides Commission also solicited public input. To that end, Vice-Chairman Bill Thomas made a point of publicizing his own e-mail address. Upon hearing that, I collated and delivered a wealth of information and material unearthed in my review and analysis of a host of regulatory reports and legal complaints. I didn't expect any sort of formal engagement by the commission, but the fact that I did not even receive a rubber-stamp acknowledgment of receipt mildly surprised me. Was the commission so hard-pressed for resources, or were Thomas and the rest merely pandering to the public?

The commission was clearly concerned that it be viewed as impartial. That concern was well founded, given that the commission itself was composed of four individuals appointed by the Republican power base in Washington and six individuals, including the chairman, appointed by the Democratic Party. The commission was charged with investigating 22 separate causes, covering almost every imaginable corner on Wall Street. Almost.

As need be, the commission had the power to subpoena in order to compel testimony and gain access to documents and information. While the bulk of the commission's efforts were directed at a wide array of practices employed on Wall Street, the commission also directed significant attention toward select financial regulators and policymakers in Washington.

As the commission prepared to launch its efforts in early 2010, public trust and confidence in Wall Street and Washington continued to wane. The increasing levels of public anxiety fueled the burgeoning Tea Party movement prior to the midterm elections that fall. The president and his staff were clearly cognizant of this public sentiment. The Federal Reserve and US Treasury continued to wield the real weight in Washington, though, via policies largely directed at recapitalizing the financial system and propping the markets in hopes of sparking the economy, which continued to be burdened with excessive debt. Their ongoing support of Wall Street during this period only further exacerbated the pain and anxiety felt by so many on Main Street.

While the American public—from the right, left, and center—was concerned with employment, declining incomes, and dispensing justice for those engaged in what most in our nation deemed to be extraordinary financial frauds, those on the right and left in Washington increasingly haggled over health-care reform proposals. The dwindling trust in our public officials was redirected squarely upon the shoulders of the members of the FCIC.

America not only wanted to learn *what* happened on Wall Street but more importantly *who* did it, *how* it went down, and *why* regulators were not able to uphold their mandate to protect investors, consumers, and the public at large.

With high hopes, the public tuned in to the FCIC's first public hearing on January 13, 2010. The bulk of that first day was directed to the questioning of Wall Street heavyweights Lloyd Blankfein of Goldman Sachs, Jamie Dimon of J.P. Morgan, John Mack of Morgan Stanley, and Brian Moynihan of Bank of America. Might the American public once again witness a banking executive summarily disgraced and discredited, as Ferdinand Pecora had done to Charles Mitchell back in 1933?

The commission's Heather Murren did land a few glancing blows during that first round as she challenged Wall Street's power base about the industry's regulatory oversight, but most lines of questioning from other commission members were parried by the bankers, well-schooled in the art of deft—if not deceptive—public speaking.

If the first round of questioning by the FCIC was underwhelming, the second day was downright disappointing. Who took their seats under the bright lights of interrogation? None other than Attorney General Eric Holder, Assistant Attorney General Lanny Breuer, FDIC chair Sheila Bair, and SEC chief (former FINRA chief) Mary Schapiro. Neither Holder nor Breuer provided any meaningful or explicit revelations. Bair did provide extensive background materials that implicated large parts of Wall Street and Washington, but she promised more than she delivered in her final statement: "The regulatory system also failed in its responsibilities. There were critical shortcomings in our approach that permitted excessive risks to build in the system. Existing authorities were not always used, regulatory gaps within the financial system provided an environment in which regulatory arbitrage became rampant, and the failure to adequately protect consumers created safety-and-soundness problems."[4]

Failed *how?* Failed *where? Which* authorities? *What* gaps?

If Bair was comprehensive but not specific, then Schapiro was little more than coy. There were few people that the FCIC might be able to interview who could provide as wide a window onto Wall Street as Mary Schapiro, given her 20-plus-year career within the wide web of financial overseers. She served stints at the SEC during the Reagan and George H. W. Bush administrations and was appointed acting chairman of the SEC by President Bill Clinton in 1993. Her subsequent move into the chairman's seat of the Commodity Futures Trading Commission distinguished her as the first person to serve as chairman of both of these financial police forces. In addition to her regulatory work over the last 25 years, she also sat on a number of governmental financial oversight and stability boards. If anybody knew where a host of bones was buried on Wall Street leading up to and even after the market crash of 2008, it was Mary Schapiro.

On that second day of formal questioning by the FCIC, both the commissioners and Schapiro had every opportunity to take the public into the back alleys of Wall Street and shed light on the regulatory failures and gaps within the organizations where she had worked (FINRA, NASD, CFTC, SEC). Nobody expected Schapiro to voluntarily unearth anything meaningful, but those watching closely might have hoped for at least a few helpful clues. We got little of the sort, as her opening testimony and subsequent questions and answers provided little more than an indictment of the SEC during the Bush regime. The fact that the FCIC did not redirect Schapiro's focus and aggressively question her experience and tenure at these other regulators was a telltale sign that Angelides and team bore little resemblance to Ferdinand Pecora.

The FCIC did score some points with the public when Richard Bowen, former chief underwriter of Citigroup's consumer lending group, testified. Unlike many of the financial executives and regulatory and judicial officials who took a naturally defensive posture in their testimony, Bowen quickly went on the offensive. In what could only be described as a bombshell, Bowen highlighted that he had determined in mid-2006 that more than 60 percent of the mortgages that Citi had purchased from third-party originators and sold to investors such as Freddie Mac and Fannie Mae were defective—that is, they did not meet Citi's standards. Bowen sent messages to senior Citi management, including former US Treasury secretary Robert Rubin, indicating the seriousness of this matter and the urgency with which it needed to be addressed, but his whistleblowing fell upon deaf ears. Bowen also testified that in 2007, the defective mortgages purchased by Citi increased to over 80 percent.

If Citi was experiencing a 60 percent defective rate within its mortgage pipeline, what percentage of defective mortgages were actual frauds? And what were the larger mortgage players (Countrywide, JPMorgan Chase, Wells Fargo, Wachovia, Washington Mutual, and Bank of America) experiencing in terms of defective or fraudulently underwritten mortgages?

Further indication that the FCIC was heading down the right path in this pursuit was the fact that Bowen, like the proverbial canary in the coal mine, had lost his job at Citi in early 2009 after having blown the whistle within the bank. This further whetted the public appetite for a Pecora-like discrediting of one of Wall Street and Washington's most powerful executives, as Robert Rubin and former Citi CEO Chuck Prince prepared to face the music on the very next day.

Prince was expressly apologetic to the FCIC, while Rubin bobbed and weaved with the best of them. Despite being given every advantage from Bowen's testimony, the high-browed volleys launched by Angelides and Thomas upon Rubin failed to unnerve him. Rubin, like many other Wall Street executives, fell back upon the convenient excuse that powerful forces had come together in a perfect storm to overwhelm Wall Street and America. That excuse, proffered along with an oft-mentioned "I do not recall," stonewalled any meaningful line of questioning. Increasingly, the commission's one step forward, two steps sideways, and one step back was sapping whatever momentum they had.

The public testimony and questioning of Bear Stearns CEO Jimmy Cayne was of little value. The once proud, if not arrogant, executive now appeared weathered and beaten. His abbreviated answers evoked some sympathy, but more impatience, as he conveyed a lack of meaningful understanding of the issues. Cayne's terse responses were of little help.

The questioning of former Fannie Mae CEO Daniel Mudd was similarly uneventful and only served as a reminder that former Fannie executives Franklin Raines, Jim Johnson, and Tim Howard were not even on the stand. Raines, Johnson, and Howard had few equals in currying and dispensing favors in both Wall Street and Washington. Raines and Howard unceremoniously departed from Fannie Mae in 2004 after Fannie's books were deemed to have been cooked. Johnson was forced out under questionable circumstances surrounding his compensation. He briefly served on President Obama's vice-presidential search team until he was viewed more as a liability than an asset.

As it continued its work, the FCIC issued a subpoena against Goldman Sachs for refusing to divulge information, including documents detailing its controversial bets within the mortgage market. This action garnered a bit of temporary goodwill for the FCIC, but no permanent change in the public opinion that Wall Street ultimately answered to nobody but itself.

Unlike the Pecora Investigation, the FCIC generated no grand conquests or exposés during the course of its work. But at least the final report did not accept the "perfect storm" excuse put forth by so many on Wall Street.

> We conclude this financial crisis was avoidable. The crisis was the result of human action and inaction, not of Mother Nature or computer models gone haywire. The captains of finance and the public stewards of our financial system ignored warnings and failed to question, understand, and manage evolving risks within a system essential to the well-being of the American public. Theirs

was a big miss, not a stumble. While the business cycle cannot be repealed, a crisis of this magnitude need not have occurred. To paraphrase Shakespeare, the fault lies not in the stars, but in us.

Despite the expressed view of many on Wall Street and in Washington that the crisis could not have been foreseen or avoided, there were warning signs. The tragedy was that they were ignored or discounted.[5]

The final report ran 633 pages and did probe deeply into a host of issues that brought our markets and economy crashing down. One compelling clue to explain *how* the crisis happened was found on page 53 of the report: "Former Securities and Exchange Commission chairman Arthur Levitt told the FCIC that once word of a proposed regulation got out, industry lobbyists would rush to complain to members of the congressional committee with jurisdiction over the financial activity at issue. According to Levitt, these members would then "harass" the SEC with frequent letters demanding answers to complex questions and appearances of officials before Congress. These requests consumed much of the agency's time and discouraged it from making regulations. Levitt described it as "kind of a blood sport to make the particular agency look stupid or inept or venal."[6]

Clearly, the members of Congress were doing the bidding of the industry rather than working on behalf of the public. Yet we never learned *which* members of Congress were most guilty of this harassment, nor did we learn if or how *quid pro quo* was at work in this process.

While we learned much from the commission, partisan politics dominated the final report like it dominates most other efforts around Washington. Rather than rising above the fray and directing specific blame upon those individuals and institutions clearly responsible for massive failures to perform, the FCIC fell short of its ultimate mission and played politics, pointing the fingers at failed policies and programs along party lines. As the dissenting statement provided by the commissioners aligned with the Republican Party indicated, "In the end, the majority's report turned out to be a just so story *about* the financial crisis, rather than a report on what *caused* the financial crisis."[7]

Pecora would not have been impressed. Nor was FCIC commissioner Keith Hennessey, who informed me the FCIC's work was "not a great success." Subsequent to the FCIC's final report, more mudslinging from both sides of the aisle showed Congress to be more concerned with scoring political points than actually getting at the full and unbridled truth.

A year after the FCIC's final report was issued, the one real star of the show, Citi's Richard Bowen, unleashed another volley that only furthered the public's lack of confidence in the system. Close to two years after providing his hard-hitting testimony to the FCIC, Bowen revealed that "the commission directed him to delete his most serious charge, that Citigroup managers knew but never warned company stakeholders who had invested in funds backed by the risky" mortgages.[8]

With this admission, Bowen pulled back the covers on a massive fraud. To know that loans backing an investment fund are defective—if not completely fraudulent—and to go forth with the offering regardless would not pass muster in any courtroom and certainly not in the court of public opinion. This sort of revelation was exactly what the American public was salivating for, and would have provided a wealth of ammo for the commissioners to direct at Prince and Rubin the next day. But the breath of truth, transparency, and integrity that Bowen could have provided remained stifled.

Citigroup certainly had plenty of experience in packaging and distributing defective mortgages. Late in 2011, the bank agreed to a not-insignificant settlement of $285 million for betting against its clients and investors in a $1 billion housing-related transaction. A judge subsequently rejected that settlement on the premise that the bank should not have been able to write a check even of that size while "neither admitting nor denying" the details of the case. Very few jurists have been willing to reject these settlements that incorporate the practice of foisting a fine onto the backs of shareholders while simultaneously allowing executives to skate free.

Bowen's statements both during and after the commission hearings are strong indications that Angelides and team were working at the behest of higher powers in Washington. What drove these powers? Clearly they were more concerned with managing the flow of information and protecting selected individuals, firms, and agencies than restoring the trust and confidence of the American public. If the FCIC was willing to muzzle Bowen, then perhaps it is no surprise that, despite public calls, they forsook the opportunity to look into Wall Street's largest self-regulatory organization, FINRA.

Specifically, the Alliance for Economic Stability—a nonpartisan economic policy organization established to encourage policies that protect savings and investments and promote a fair financial marketplace—called on the FCIC to investigate FINRA. In a delivery eerily reminiscent to the testimony provided by Harry Markopolos atop Capitol Hill, the AES wrote:

> Little known to most Americans, FINRA is the nation's largest financial regulator and the organization with the most direct day-to-day oversight of financial firms. However, FINRA has garnered no visible attention from legislators and other government officials as they consider changes to the financial regulatory system.

Most recently, FINRA has evaded scrutiny for having failed to uncover the Lehman Brothers Repo 105 program. FINRA's most direct and specific responsibility is to supervise a firm's compliance with capital requirements. FINRA failed not just in Lehman, but Bear Stearns and AIG as well, yet has not been the subject of any investigative action.

Meanwhile FINRA executives use court-granted immunity and a lack of oversight to enrich themselves, making fortunes as what can only be described as "rogue cops."[9]

With Bowen largely silenced and FINRA not even inspected, the public increasingly sensed that the fix was in. They knew the crisis that centered on Wall Street encompassed a host of fraudulent activities in the origination, securitization, distribution, and hedging of mortgage-related products, among other illicit activities.

The behavior of selected individuals and institutions needs to be exposed and properly adjudicated if capitalism is to exorcise the cronyism that was core to the fraud. James K. Galbraith, the chair in government and business relations at the University of Texas at Austin, understood this. Galbraith addressed the Senate Judiciary Committee's Subcommittee on Crime in mid-2010 and laid out the shortcomings behind and the fallout from our economic crisis. His exquisitely detailed testimony skewered his own profession, the study of economic theory, for its failure to properly delve into and understand systemic financial frauds. In point of fact, leading into the current crisis, Wall Street curried favor with academics by paying them to produce research supportive of practices and market developments central to the perpetuation of fraud.

Galbraith methodically detailed the manner in which a control fraud—when a trusted person in a position of responsibility subverts the system/company for personal gain—develops, flourishes, perpetuates, and ultimately fails. The failure of the fraud, though, belies the fact that many of the perpetrators walk away filthy rich. The fraud itself and the injustice running throughout the system are predicated on a failure of the rule of law in mandating and upholding legal contracts. These failures have been propagated by our government, regulators, ratings agencies, a wide array of financial institutions, and individual citizens as well. As frauds go unpunished and moral hazards propagate, our nation has seemingly become inured to the growth of other frauds and moral hazards. We have seen evidence of this dynamic in areas like union-dominated pension schemes and personal consumer behaviors, including the intentional nonpayment of debts with the expectation of not being penalized. Just as banks were bailed out, an unhealthy "bail me out too" mentality has taken hold in our nation. What is the end result? The abuse of capitalism persists unabated under the guise that every criticism threatens to tear down the economy, and every measure of support for our economy is prioritized over upholding our legal system let alone embracing a sense of moral decency. Galbraith harkened back to a period in our nation's history when a sense of decency and meaningful justice for all was central to our national fabric: "Some fraud is inevitable, but in a functioning system it must be rare. It must be considered—and rightly—a minor problem. If fraud—or even the perception of fraud—comes to dominate the system, then there is no foundation for a market in the securities. They become trash. And more deeply, so do the institutions responsible for creating, rating and selling them. Including, so long as it fails to respond with appropriate force, the legal system itself."[10]

Galbraith understands and shared that no amount of support provided by the Federal Reserve or any other governmental or private entity can disguise the inestimable price borne by our society from a deeply buried yet unpunished control fraud. The monetary value associated with this price pales in comparison to the national decline in trust felt by a citizenry disgusted by those who have continually failed to uphold the rule of law: "In this situation, let me suggest, the country faces an existential threat. Either the legal system must do its work. Or the market system cannot be restored. There must be a thorough, transparent, effective, radical cleaning of the financial sector and also of those public officials who failed the public trust. The financiers must be made to feel, in their bones, the power of the law. And the public, which lives by the law, must see very clearly and unambiguously that this is the case."[11]

Galbraith would have impressed Pecora. Yet Congress and the Department of Justice have largely failed to act upon Galbraith's recommendations. Galbraith was not the only one directing the FCIC and Congress to act. While the FCIC was engaged in what ultimately looked like shadowboxing, others with extensive background in exposing shady financial dealings were also speaking out and impelling Congress to look hard at FINRA, most notably, the longstanding proponents of transparency at the Project on Government Oversight (POGO).

Well positioned in Washington and with unquestioned credibility, POGO delivered Congress a detailed road map of FINRA, outlining numerous concerns in a February 2010 letter to the House Committee on Financial Services, the House Committee on Oversight and Government Reform, the Senate Committee on Banking, Housing, & Urban Affairs, and the Senate Committee on Finance:

1. **FINRA has attempted to expand its authority despite its abysmal track record.** In scaling a bar held barely inches off the ground, "FINRA Chairman and CEO Richard Ketchum testified that FINRA should be given the authority to

oversee investment advisers in addition to securities broker-age firms. In an attempt to justify this expanded authority, Ketchum argued that FINRA has a 'strong track record in our examination and enforcement oversight.'"[12]

2. **Regulators awarded executives outrageous compensation packages, even during the height of the crisis.** "Tax documents show that in 2008—a year in which FINRA also lost $568 million in its investment portfolio—the organization's 20 senior executives received nearly $30 million in salaries and bonuses."[13]

3. **FINRA failed to warn the public about ARS.**

4. **The incestuous relationship between FINRA and the Securities Industry,** as exemplified in the complaints brought on behalf of Amerivet Securities, Standard Investment Chartered, and Benchmark Financial, and in the well-oiled revolving door between FINRA and a host of industry-related firms.

5. **Investors and taxpayers have been forced to foot the bill for regulatory ineptness or malfeasance.** The direct and indirect costs of which are incalculable given the trillions of dollars in bailouts and the pain caused by our ongoing economic crisis.

6. **It is now time to challenge the government's reliance on SROs.** Given the inherent conflicts of interest in the financial self-regulatory model, one is hard pressed to accept the efficacy of just such a system, and as such, "POGO calls on Congress to consider vastly curtailing the power of SROs."[14]

With all of those landmines within FINRA, to think that the FCIC totally overlooked this organization speaks volumes as to how deeply the commission really cared about looking for the root causes of our economic crisis.

One would think these four major congressional committees would have to weigh in with some sort of opinion on such a detailed appeal as that put forth by POGO. But with the bulk of the issues within POGO's letter still unresolved and the crisis enduring, the American public is left wondering if POGO's letter was even read by those atop Capitol Hill. POGO's Michael Smallberg informed me, "No one from the committees responded to our 2010 letter. But we did hear from a number of investors, shareholders, reporters, and securities brokers who told us about a host of problems at FINRA."

Of course, most of the American public has little understanding or appreciation for the impact a massively conflicted financial self-regulatory model has upon their lives. That said, one would hope and expect that our elected representatives sitting on committees charged with financial oversight would be well versed in the issues relating to this topic. Do not be so sure. Smallberg works deeply within these spheres and offered a stinging rebuke of some on the aforementioned committees in stating that he "suspects there are some committee members who have never even heard of FINRA." That assessment is certainly disappointing but not overly surprising given the general lack of meaningful financial intelligence displayed by congressional members in a variety of Wall Street related hearings.

Given the strength of POGO's letter, one might have thought it would have generated a response from FINRA's overseers at the SEC. Whether the SEC was even aware of the letter or not, the simple fact is when it comes to sharing information, the SEC plays its cards very close to the vest. Smallberg alluded to as much: "POGO has raised concerns about SEC officials who used to work for FINRA and the SEC's use of a FOIA [Freedom of Information

Act] exemption to withhold information about the agency's oversight of FINRA." The secretive nature of these organizations has done absolutely nothing to help regenerate any sense of meaningful trust and confidence in the system. Nor should anybody think that the closed door policy within FINRA and the SEC will change anytime soon. As with many other issues of importance in and around Washington, we learn from Smallberg that "Congress kicked the can down the road on the issue of self-regulation" and that Dodd-Frank legislated that Congress merely "required the SEC to study the issue." Given the Federal Reserve's predilection to postpone if not outright derail many aspects of meaningful financial reforms within the Dodd-Frank legislation, the prospect that the self-regulatory model will receive meaningful attention strikes me as a pipe dream.

Life on Wall Street and in Washington may go on, but the world remains unsettled. Increasingly, people are so discouraged about employment opportunities that they have stopped looking for work altogether, overall economic growth remains anemic, and more and more people struggle to make ends meet. Trust remains in very short supply, for as Smallberg summarizes, "Recent scandals in the financial industry, including the manipulation of Libor, have only heightened our suspicion that large financial institutions cannot be trusted to regulate themselves. The need for Congress to investigate FINRA and the model of self-regulation has never been stronger. Anyone who cares about the independence, transparency, and accountability of our federal regulatory system should make the oversight of FINRA a top priority."

FINRA was referenced three times in the midst of the 633-page FCIC report. Two of the references were in the index, and one reference was made to a situation regarding the allocation of initial public offerings in the year 2000. With such little attention paid to FINRA by both the FCIC and Congress, many would not guess that this organization was so close to ground zero for the ultimate market meltdown and the greatest ongoing economic crisis of the last 75 years.

Pecora would not have been impressed.

ELEVEN
TOO BIG TO REGULATE

Dodd Frank also gives regulators a variety of mechanisms they can use to channel political policy through the dominant institutions. The partnership works in both directions: special treatment for the Wall Street giants, new political policy levers for the government.

—David Skeel, S. Samuel Arsht Professor of Corporate Law,

University of Pennsylvania Law School,

The New Financial Deal:

Understanding the Dodd-Frank Act

and Its (Unintended) Consequences

AFTER 2008, THE NUMBER OF BROKERAGE HOUSES ON Wall Street significantly diminished. No longer did the names Bear Stearns, Lehman Brothers, Wachovia, Countrywide, Washington Mutual, and Merrill Lynch represent single-standing entities. While most of these houses were taken over by other firms at the behest of Uncle Sam, the fire that engulfed the house of Lehman threatened all the other financial houses and the world economy were it not for the liquidity of Uncle Sam's bailout.

The Wall Street landscape was greatly changed. In order to appreciate how business operates among the remaining houses, we need to understand the dynamics of a sparsely populated neighborhood.

Not long ago, Wall Street had far more houses than just those that fell in the crisis. The truth is, there have been an extraordinary amount of takeovers and consolidations on Wall Street over the last few decades. In the process, many legendary houses have been relegated to little more than footnotes in Wall Street lore: A.G. Becker; Alex Brown; A.G. Edwards; Bankers Trust; Dillon Read; Dean Witter; Donaldson, Lufkin & Jenrette; Drexel Burnham; E.F. Hutton; First Boston; First Union; Greenwich Capital; Hambrecht & Quist; Kidder Peabody & Co.; Kuhn, Loeb & Co.; Irving Trust; Montgomery; Nations Bank; Paine Webber; Prudential Securities; Robertson Stephens; Salomon Brothers; Shearson; Swiss Bank; Warburg; Wertheim; and more.

If you walk down Wall Street now, what do you see? For an industry that once boasted a wide array of large, medium, and small houses, Wall Street now is dominated by a handful of megabanks, including Goldman Sachs, JPMorgan Chase, Citigroup, Bank of America, Morgan Stanley, and Wells Fargo. Foreign houses include Barclays, Deutsche Bank, Credit Suisse, Royal Bank of Scotland, HSBC, and Union Bank of Switzerland. Although there are plenty of other houses that operate within the financial markets, these sprawling firms can flex their muscles and exert uncommon, if not unhealthy, influence.

If Wall Street was once the embodiment of free market capitalism, the new neighborhood is nothing short of an oligopoly—that is, a system in which markets are dominated by a small number of firms. Typical behaviors often witnessed within an oligopoly include:

- Price controls, periodic bouts of collusion, and market manipulation.
- Barriers to entry are kept very high.
- Firms can retain abnormally high profits long term.

- Firms can and will hoard and withhold information and knowledge.
- Those individuals and institutions outside the system do not have access to the information and knowledge and pay the price literally and figuratively in the process.
- A high degree of interdependence among the firms.
- Conflicts of interest are accentuated as opportunities arise to deal in a proprietary manner as opposed to engaging in customer-related business.

Not exactly a healthy system for anyone outside of the inner circle. An oligopoly is also not ideal for investors and consumers. Away from Wall Street, we also see oligopolies at work within aircraft manufacturing, media, wireless communications, film and television production, oil and gas, and the mining of selected metals.

While Wall Street certainly had oligopolistic tendencies well before the recent crisis, the trend has sharply accelerated in the last few years. In fact, as the government has looked to help the banking system recapitalize itself, there is no doubt that the megabanks have taken advantage of the less competitive marketplace. Just consider the following evidence:

- Numerous quarterly reporting periods in which the large banks have literally generated profits each and every day. These perfect scores, so to speak, were unheard of under normal market conditions.
- Exceptional collateral demands made by the banks of their customers engaging in derivatives transactions. As highlighted by *Bloomberg*: "Goldman Sachs Group Inc. and JPMorgan Chase & Co., two of the biggest traders of over-the-counter derivatives, are exploiting their growing

clout in that market to secure cheap funding in addition to billions in revenue from the business. . . . 'If you're seen as a major player and you have a product that people can't get elsewhere, you have the negotiating power,' said Richard Lindsey, a former director of market regulation at the U.S. Securities and Exchange Commission who ran the prime brokerage unit at Bear Stearns Cos. from 1999 to 2006."[1]

- Investment banking fees for underwriting activities, mergers and acquisitions, and advisory work are high, and often the work presents conflicts of interest for firms that maintain both proprietary investment and trading operations.

- The disingenuous manner in which the large banks engaged homeowners attempting to modify their mortgages. The mortgage servicing arms of these large banks are supposed to work on behalf of homeowners and investors. Illicit practices by servicers across the industry, including the robo-signing of mortgage documents within foreclosure proceedings, gave the appearance of collusive racketeering and led to multi-billion dollar settlements.

- The ability for the megabanks to utilize their competitive advantage from the implied government-subsidized "too big to fail" funding of operations allows them to squeeze other firms right out. This lessened competition yields higher transaction costs across a wide array of products for investors and consumers alike.

Across virtually every line of business on Wall Street, from trading to consumer lending, we are seeing profiteering from collusive-type pricing. In certain circumstances, such as the manipulation of overnight interest rates (e.g., Libor) that was widely exposed in

2012, the collusion was clearly illegal. In other instances, such as the ongoing exorbitant interest rates on credit cards, the practices were technically legal, but the end results (outsized profits and little competition) were very much the same. After the bailout, the once "too big to fail" banks sitting high atop the hill on Wall Street have now only gotten that much bigger:

- The four largest mortgage originators (Wells Fargo, JP Morgan Chase, U.S. Bancorp, and Bank of America) now write approximately 50 percent of the home mortgages in our country. The largest originator, Wells Fargo, has approximately 30 percent of the market.
- The four largest banks issue close to 70 percent of the credit cards.
- The six largest banks by assets (JPMorgan Chase, Bank of America, Citigroup, Wells Fargo, Goldman Sachs, and Morgan Stanley) hold assets valued at close to two-thirds of our nation's GDP. In 1995 the six largest banks held assets equal to 17 percent of our nation's GDP.
- The four largest banks hold close to 40 percent of our nation's bank deposits, up from 32 percent pre-crisis.[2]

If there was ever a doubt that our megabanks were "too big to fail," then this final piece of data, the granddaddy of them all, will defy those who might believe otherwise:

- The five largest banks hold 95 percent of the exposure within the quadrillion-dollar (that is a thousand trillion) derivatives market. That figure represents approximately $3.2 million for every man, woman, and child in the United

States of America. The banks dominating this market sector are JPMorgan Chase, Bank of America, Citigroup, Wells Fargo, and Goldman Sachs.[3]

And of course, under the "too big to fail" business model, these banks have also become "too big to regulate." Many Wall Street executives, especially J.P. Morgan's Jamie Dimon, would deny this assertion. However, J.P. Morgan's $6 billion loss due to derivatives trading activity within its chief investment office in 2012 says otherwise. Not to allow their advantages to go to waste, the banks and their executives have been able to position themselves as "too big to prosecute" as well.

Against the backdrop of populist rage directed at Wall Street, Washington knew that it needed to bring some form of renewed regulatory oversight to an industry that had lost its moral compass— if not its way entirely. The legislation undertaken was designated the Dodd-Frank Wall Street Reform and Consumer Protection Act, given that it was led by Senator Christopher Dodd (D-CT) and Representative Barney Frank (D-MA). Dodd chaired the Senate Banking Committee and Frank led the House Financial Services Committee. Given those positions, it was not a surprise that they would have led the legislative effort to reform Wall Street; however, for those who watched closely, it seemed all too surreal that two individuals who had long fed sumptuously at the Wall Street (and related) troughs were now charged with cleaning up the mess.

The stated goals of the Dodd-Frank legislation were "to promote the financial stability of the United States by improving accountability and transparency in the financial system, to end 'too big to fail,' to protect the American taxpayer by ending bailouts, to protect consumers from abusive financial services practices, and for other purposes."⁴ Certainly an all-encompassing canvas, but goals and aims are one thing; the delivery and impact of the law rest in the details and implementation.

As with any sweeping piece of legislation, political pressures and heavy lobbying are to be expected from groups not looking to cede previously hard-won turf battles. Few groups knew how to play that game better than the Wall Street lobby that had funneled billions of dollars into the campaign war chests of Washington legislators.

A year's worth of debate, political maneuvering, and assorted machinations from a wide array of constituencies ultimately yielded a Dodd-Frank bill that ran more than 2,300 pages. Many in Washington heralded the legislation as bringing the requisite reforms to an industry that had developed and launched financial weapons of mass destruction. Truth be told, the act was more an architectural blueprint subject to further review, analysis, and revision than a finished product ready to return our markets and economy to healthy footing.

Aside from the thousands of pages of actual text, Dodd-Frank directed no less than 22 separate regulators to undertake work on over 400 separate rules. These regulators encompassed not only existing agencies but also newly formed entities such as the Financial Stability Oversight Council and the Consumer Financial Protection Bureau. The former was charged with identifying and managing systemic risk in the financial system. The latter was directed to make markets for consumer financial products and services work for Americans. Existing institutions deeply affected by the new legislation are the Commodity Futures Trading Commission (CFTC), Department of Treasury, Federal Deposit Insurance Corporation, Federal Housing Finance Agency, Federal Reserve, Federal Energy Regulatory Commission, Federal Trade Commission, National Credit Union Administration, Office of the Comptroller of the

Currency, Office of Thrift Supervision, State Insurance Regulator, and the Securities and Exchange Commission.

Not many folks seemed to notice that there was no meaningful mention of the Wall Street-funded police known as the Financial Industry Regulatory Authority included in this legislation, despite its ostensible mission of bringing financial regulatory reform to Wall Street.

Conspicuously absent was substantial discussion of the political leaders and regulators who manned our ship while it crashed on the rocks, and were now peddling reform from the pulpit. The United States Chamber of Commerce brought attention to this pathetic reality. "The Dodd-Frank Act left nearly every pre-crisis regulator intact and failed to address longstanding, fundamental weaknesses in the system. While increasing the workloads of the existing agencies, the Act did not introduce the critical infrastructural and process changes within agencies needed to restore regulatory efficiency and effectiveness."[5]

The enormous symbolic tarpaulin presented by Dodd-Frank promised unknown yet widespread new regulations and serious hurdles for chief financial officers and other executives involved in business planning. Many of these executives felt they were paying the price for bad practices that were centered on Wall Street, even if their business was far removed, literally and figuratively, from our nation's financial hub. Regulatory uncertainty is not conducive to economic growth, but that is what we got when legislators, bank executives, and lobbyists came together. In the process, the ties that bind Wall Street and Washington have grown even tighter. Accountability and transparency in the financial system? Nice buzzwords for politicians and regulators pandering to the public, but not when the all-powerful Federal Reserve is holding court behind closed doors to finesse the finer points raised by Dodd-Frank.

Washington continues to extol Dodd-Frank as the means by which our financial industry is being cleaned up, but this is largely a bill of goods. The legislation is the architectural outline, but the engineers working on the opaque operation are largely based within the Federal Reserve. As the *Wall Street Journal* highlighted in early 2012, "While many Americans may not realize it, the Fed has taken on a much larger regulatory role than at any time in history."[6]

During the critical first few years after the passage of Dodd-Frank, when much of the research and analysis for proposed reforms was being undertaken, the calendars of Fed, Treasury, and CFTC officials were overwhelmingly filled by meetings with representatives of the major Wall Street banks. No surprise there. These lobbyists certainly knew their way around Washington. Why bother forming an oligopoly unless one takes advantage of the perks?[7]

Those meetings, often led by Federal Reserve Chairman Ben Bernanke himself, have spawned wide-ranging legal and practical changes to the financial industry with little to no public input. In so many words, investors and consumers are being told by the Fed, "Trust us on this." Imagine the nerve—the very entity that was at the wheel of the nation's economy as it lurched into the ditch continues not only to hold the keys but to steer in the most favorable direction for its banking brethren. The rest of the American populace is simply carried along as excess baggage.

Did Dodd-Frank succeed in addressing its key goal, that is, did this massive piece of regulatory reform categorically end "too big to fail"? In print or theory perhaps, but in practice Dodd-Frank has set a course that tries to establish a price tag, underwritten by the large systemically important financial institutions, for the "too big to fail" subsidy provided by Uncle Sam. This price, in terms of increased capital ratios, may or may not ultimately lessen the risk or costs of future bailouts, but it certainly does not eliminate the possibility of them.

Most individuals in Washington and elsewhere have acknowledged that while we might hope to work our way back toward true capitalism and allow major banks to fail, we are still a long way from that reality. To state otherwise, regulators and public officials would open themselves up to ridicule. "Not even the Secretary of the Treasury, Timothy Geithner, believes that the Dodd-Frank Act ended 'too big to fail.' When asked . . . Secretary Geithner said out loud what everyone already knows to be the truth: 'In the future we may have to do exceptional things again if we face a shock that large.'"[8]

On the topic of protecting consumers, the jury remains out as to how effective the CFPB may be in minimizing predatory practices. There is real concern that the legislation may be impinging heavily upon smaller providers of credit, while the large banks can easily pass along the same increased costs to consumers.

In regard to protecting investors, there is an initiative within Dodd-Frank that addresses the fact that the SEC plans on implementing an investor advocacy effort to alleviate the growing sense of betrayal among investors toward financial regulators who clearly failed them. This effort has received little to no meaningful attention. A recent court ruling that the SEC could not be held liable for its failure to protect investors in the Madoff scandal sent a much louder message than this advocacy effort ever could.

The lingering question for so many investors and consumers is, how and why has there been little meaningful justice delivered to what were clearly egregious acts of fraud during the economic crisis? While the SEC has tried to repair its image after failing to protect investors, those watching closely know that meaningful investor protection on Wall Street is best measured by: access to information, quality of work executed by the police on the beat, and embracing and protecting whistleblowers. The current readings of these indicators suggest more turbulent times ahead. Although the SEC claims that a new day has dawned within the organization, the long shadows cast by career regulators all too familiar with past practices presents a hurdle far higher than Washington has ever even attempted to scale.

The SEC has never fully embraced the Freedom of Information Act (FOIA). Shortly after the crisis, the SEC's own inspector general reported that the commission complied with FOIA requests only 10 percent of the time and responded at a rate typically three times slower than other federal agencies.

Tellingly, the initial draft of Dodd-Frank actually included a sweeping FOIA exemption for the SEC that would have meaningfully inhibited access to information within the SEC. The legislation was amended only after a publicly embarrassing expose of this reality by *Fox Business*.[9] If the exemption had remained in place, the pursuit and ultimate justice driven by Gary Aguirre in the Pequot insider trading scandal never could have happened.

Despite utilizing a legal cover of immunity typically only accorded to governmental agencies, Wall Street's private police force at FINRA is exempt from the Freedom of Information Act. To add further insult to that injury, for purposes of a FOIA exemption, the SEC regards FINRA as a financial institution rather than a regulator. As such, the doors to information about FINRA largely remain closed.[10]

On the performance front, the SEC's failures to perform on the Madoff and Stanford cases—among others—indicate system-wide failings within the organization. Evidence of shoddy record-keeping within the commission were mere previews to allegations highlighted in an internal whistleblower suit brought by the SEC's then-assistant inspector general David Weber. The shocking charges included: sleeping around within the SEC Inspector General's Office; pay-to-play arrangements; and SEC Commissioner Mary Schapiro lying during congressional testimony.[11] Weber was vindicated, and in mid-2013 he received close to $600,000 in settlement.[12] Five-plus years after the nation initially learned of the ineptitude of the SEC, Weber's case shows the SEC to be an agency still in need of a real makeover—and some still suggest it needs to be scrapped completely.

FINRA had its own failings in dealing with both the Madoff and Stanford affairs, as well. Aside from those highly publicized failures to protect investors, FINRA has benefited from the focus on its overseers the SEC, deflecting attention away from its own performance. In 2012, an industry newsletter recognized FINRA's anniversary and reported, "In the five years since, the independent regulator of brokers has brought 6,291 disciplinary actions and levied fines totaling $254.1 million."[13]

The 6,291 disciplinary actions brought over five years equates to 1,258 cases per year. With approximately 250 business days per year, FINRA has brought five cases for every business day during its existence. They are obviously busy writing a lot of tickets. Over the course of five years $254.1 million in fines were levied, which equates to $50.8 million per year—not exactly a meaningful figure. For an industry in which the five largest firms set aside over $90 billion to pay employees in 2012 alone, the $50.8 million in fines collected by FINRA is a statistically insignificant sum. Little wonder why Wall Street welcomes being a self-regulated industry.

FINRA's largest single fine ever levied was a $12 million penalty assessed to the Union Bank of Switzerland for activities commonly connected to a destructive trading practice defined as naked short selling. While $12 million in absolute terms may be viewed as a significant sum of money by the uninformed, a $12 million fine on

Wall Street for an activity of this sort is more akin to a slap on the back from an accomplice than a kick in the pants from a real cop. UBS's transgressions in this practice occurred during a period covering more than five years and "extrapolating from the quantified violations indicated that the firm likely mismarked tens of millions of sale orders."[14]

A quick back-of-the-envelope calculation indicates that FINRA's fine imposed upon UBS equated to an approximate charge of less than $1.20 per violation. Yes, that is accurate. Not even one dollar and twenty cents per violation. Be mindful that this was the *largest* fine FINRA imposed during its first five years of existence.

For those watching closely, any semblance of integrity remaining within this self-regulatory organization was extinguished after that data point was revealed. FINRA writes on average five fines, or tickets, a day against the banks and brokers with an average overall penalty per ticket of approximately $40,640. These details mean one thing: The FINRA police are little more than meter maids.

This information may help explain why trading volumes have declined so precipitously, as investors have shied away from dealing with Wall Street after the crisis. But it does little to rebuild the investor and consumer trust and confidence needed to grow our economy. The FINRA "meter maid" madness may also explain why the Government Accountability Office recently recommended that the SEC improve its oversight of FINRA.[15]

If the private police from FINRA were acting as meter maids, who might be able to provide leads to expose meaningful improprieties on Wall Street? Whistleblowers. While we have already learned that the whistles were largely silent on Wall Street for the better part of the last two decades, Dodd-Frank did incorporate a new whistleblower program for the SEC. On the surface the new program is a positive step toward more rigorous oversight, but, as with much reform legislation, the theory of the act means little unless the practice is robust. Gary Aguirre shared the following riveting insights with me on the whistleblower provisions within Dodd-Frank:

The Dodd Frank Act had two types of provisions relating to whistleblowers: the whistleblower incentive provisions and enhanced protections for whistleblowers. Though it could have been stronger, e.g., a jury in whistleblower reprisal cases, the provisions were excellent. In effect, D-F deputized all employees of financial institutions regulated by the SEC and public companies to step forward with hard evidence of securities violations. It incentivizes them to do so, providing for awards ranging from 10 percent to 30 percent of the funds recovered by the SEC. It also granted them greater protections from reprisals.

However, while the SEC has received thousands of tips, it has only granted two token whistleblower awards since Dodd-Frank became law in July 2010. The failure to make awards is a disincentive for whistleblowers to step forward. Further, the SEC has outsourced its investigations of whistleblower complaints to the companies suspected of committing violations. When the SEC gets involved with a large financial institution or public company, it typically informs the suspected violators of the allegations and lets the violator retain counsel of its choice to conduct the investigation. Not surprisingly, the suspected violator's counsel finds the securities laws were not violated. Given that the SEC has chosen to make almost no awards, there is little motivation for whistleblowers inside of the public company or financial institution to risk his or her career by stepping forward.

Can this possibly be true? In layman's terms, Aguirre is saying the cops (that is, the SEC) inform the suspects (that is, the banks) of information it has collected about potential violations. In the process, the SEC allows and possibly even encourages the company to undergo a self-review in conjunction with its own counsel of the matter under question. Depending on the nature of the transgression, the company can determine what actually transpired and how it may want to proceed. Do not think for a second that the company does not undertake a review to determine where and how the SEC may have garnered its information. Recall the experience of Peter Sivere at J.P. Morgan to understand how whistleblowers might feel about playing ball with the SEC while continuing to work within an organization. Yet here we learn that the SEC is going right back to the company and informing them of the suspected violation.

Aguirre's explanation provides one answer to the question so many in our nation continue to ask, that is, how and why have the Wall Street banks been able to escape individual executive prosecutions if not criminal indictments of the entire institution?

US Attorney Preet Bharara and then-SEC enforcement director Robert Khuzami offered their own takes on these cooperative initiatives between the SEC and Department of Justice at the Practicing Law Institute's 42nd Annual Institute on Securities Regulation conference in New York. When subsequently confronted on the discussion at this conference, Khuzami was understandably defensive regarding his statement about the propriety of just such an arrangement. That said, the effective result of the cooperation between the SEC and DOJ has been a number of fines levied on Wall Street banks with next to no indictments and prosecutions of fraudulent behaviors. What is the additional lubricant that greased these wheels? Evidence indicates that the payoff for many legal eagles within the regulatory and judicial offices is a spin through the revolving door to a plum job at a law firm representing major financial clients or within the chief counsel's office of these institutions. Khuzami, himself, landed at the high profile law firm Kirkland &

Ellis LLP with a $5 million a year contract after having departed the SEC.[16]

Aside from the excessively collegial engagement between the banks, the SEC, FINRA, other regulators, and the Department of Justice, the lack of criminal prosecutions is also clear evidence that judicial officials are concerned about collateral damage to the banks as a whole and, beyond that, to the economy. This supposed "first, do no harm" cover completes the circle: The "too big to fail" institutions are not only too big to regulate but are now also deemed too big to prosecute, degrading the rule of law in our nation.

The ultimate outcome of this financial, regulatory, legislative, and judicial morass is systemic cronyism between Wall Street and Washington, which spells disaster for an economy badly in need of capital. Without a high degree of trust and confidence that investor capital will be protected, the flow of that capital will decline—and has declined. All efforts by the Federal Reserve to the contrary, a declining flow of limited capital inherently leads to a slower pace of economic growth, limited employment prospects, and an increase in our deficit. We see evidence of these results on a monthly basis. In addition to those lousy outcomes, crony capitalism as played between the major Wall Street banks and the Washington political establishment further propagates a widening in the disparity of income levels in our nation.

What is the answer? The US Chamber of Commerce provides it. "The problem with U.S. regulation is not its quantity, but its quality. Well-run businesses depend on well-regulated markets, and no legitimate business can compete in a marketplace that is not fair and transparent. The goal should never be less or more regulation, it should be better regulation."[17]

TWELVE
CHANGING THE
SHEETS

All that is necessary for the triumph of evil is that good men do nothing.

—Edmund Burke, Irish statesman, orator,
philosopher (1729–1797)

WE ARE AT A CROSSROADS. THE FINANCIAL CHARADES perpetrated over the last few decades have pushed the American dream further and further away from the grasp of many of us. Baby boomers who looked forward to retirement are increasingly compelled to keep working or look for work later in life. Families are wondering how to finance their children's higher education without going into serious debt. Young families are burdened with elevated levels of insecurity in their jobs and incomes. Recent graduates are likely to forestall marriage and starting a family as they deal with the stress of student loans and challenging employment prospects. And even these groups are the envy of the approximately 47 million people (15 percent of our population) living in poverty and subsisting on food stamps.

We may continue to "hold these truths as self-evident, that all men are created equal, that they are endowed by their Creator with certain unalienable Rights, that among these are Life, Liberty, and the pursuit of Happiness";[1] however, simply because these truths are self-evident does not mean achieving those dreams is a foregone conclusion for future generations. As with any dream, hard work and preparation are prerequisites, but level playing fields, fair dealings, meaningful investor and consumer safeguards, the sanctity of property rights, and the implementation of the rule of law are also necessary preconditions. Without these factors aggressively upheld, the inevitable widening disparity of incomes and opportunities will create all kinds of social and civil dislocations.

The fact that any of these preconditions are in doubt is a situation most would associate with an emerging market or third world nation, not the greatest country on the face of the earth. The current crisis has so eroded national confidence in our institutions that recent surveys indicate that only one in five of us now have much confidence in our banks and major television news outlets. One in six trust the stock market, and fewer than one in seven has confidence in our congressional representatives.[2]

This decline in confidence and trust has shaken our nation to its very core.

We may look askance at nations that suffer under the tyrannical rule of despots, but just because the United States was founded upon the rule of law does not preclude us from also suffering the consequences when it is practiced without rigor. Those within our central bank, US Treasury, Department of Justice, and congressional and executive offices would clearly like to keep our nation's eyes focused squarely ahead in an attempt to regenerate the confidence and trust needed to rebuild our economy. Various political leaders, including President Barack Obama, have stated that many questionable activities on Wall Street may have been immoral and unethical but not necessarily illegal. That is neither necessarily true, nor is that good enough. We expect people in leadership positions to adhere to the spirit, not simply the letter, of the law. The fact that so many no longer feel bound by that code is why we've experienced such a decline in investor protections and regulations over the last decade.

Unfortunately, many Americans are cynical enough by now to view our big money politics and corrosive lobbying efforts as standard operating procedure. But the dollars and favors that cycle in and out of Washington come with a very heavy price. The economic crisis of 2008 was not caused by some calamitous "perfect storm," as many in Washington and on Wall Street might like us to believe. It stemmed from a methodical degradation of the rule of law, investor protections, and financial regulations over a protracted period.

The World Justice Project, an independent, nonprofit organization founded to promote the rule of law throughout the world, grades each industrialized nation on a host of factors, including limited government powers, order and security, fundamental rights, absence of corruption, open government, effective regulatory enforcement, access to civil justice, effective criminal justice, and informal justice. The leading nations of the world by this metric are New Zealand, Norway, Sweden, and Australia. The United States is far from the top, ranking in the second or third decile for most measurements. When rated against nations with similar income levels, the United States looks even worse. Consider the following representative statistical sampling of data, sourced and highlighted by the World Justice Project (scale of 0–100, with higher scores being optimal):

- Government officials sanctioned for misconduct: Australia 81, United States 66, Indonesia 59
- Government officials in the legislative branch do not use public office for private gain: Malaysia 71, United States 62, China 53

- Government regulations are effectively enforced: United Arab Emirates 69, United States 65, Russia 54
- The government does not expropriate property without adequate compensation: Canada 83, United States 64, Iran 61
- Civil justice is effectively enforced: Canada 79, Iran 69, United States 63, Albania 58
- People can access and afford civil justice: Sweden 77, China 58, Russia 54, United States 53, India 46
- Criminal system is effective in reducing criminal behavior: Finland 78, China 63, Iran 49, United States 46, India 39
- Due process of law and rights of the accused are effectively guaranteed: United Kingdom 82, Australia 81, Canada 76, United States 62, China 49
- Criminal system is impartial: China 65, United States 38, Russia 37, India 35[3]

Those statistics should make American citizens stop and ponder our place among nations. In one brief generation, America went from facilitating the fall of the Berlin Wall and the opening of Eastern Europe to ushering in the greatest post-Depression economic crisis the world has ever seen. Worse, we sealed the demise of true free market capitalism with the rise of crony capitalism, in which political and financial elites consorted, if not conspired, to profit via an array of Ponzi-style financing programs and other financial chicanery that left investors, consumers, and now taxpayers in their wake.

The development of this crony capitalism came at the expense of our constitutional principles, that we are a nation governed by laws and not men. And when it all fell apart, rather than doing the hard work of exorcising the poison, our leaders chose the path of expediency by papering over the crony cesspool with trillions of dollars in central bank liquidity. Easy monetary policy may very well be the prudent path during a deleveraging and deflationary economic period, but bailouts, combined with creating one bubble to recover from another, are not the recipe for rooting out the fraud and reconstructing the foundation needed for true economic growth.

I believe the course we must take is clear. As Harvard economist Niall Ferguson opined in a *Barron's* interview in April 2012, "When countries improve rule of law, property rights, and investor protections, and when regulation becomes more transparent and corruption reduced, there are major payoffs."[4]

America badly needs increased investment activity for organic economic growth, a meaningful decline in structural unemployment, an increase in income levels and consumer demand, and a rebounding of entrepreneurial spirit. Regrettably, all this is severely hindered by the lack of trust and confidence that is the outgrowth of the Wall Street-Washington oligopoly. Yet here we sit, after the crisis that rocked our nation and the world to the very core, and aside from some legislative window dressing, very little has changed. Future generations will judge us poorly if we fail to speak out and allow this cancer to continue its spread.

Our current cronyism is not the property of one political party or the other. As with any cancer, it does not care who it attacks or where it spreads. In the process of unearthing and exposing these crony Wall Street-Washington paths, we have come to learn that large numbers from both political parties, their well-heeled financial benefactors, and many of our financial regulators all sit on one side of the table while the general investing, consuming, and taxpaying public—along with a large percentage of Wall Street's own employees—sit on the other.

Financial institutions that are "too big to fail," combined with politicians who are too compromised to govern and regulators who are too captured and corrupted to protect, produce an incestuous cabal that is simply too big to trust.

Tea Party versus Occupy Wall Street? Republican versus Democrat? Austrian versus Keynsian? Yes, all these groups and their accompanying principles bring real substance to our ongoing policy debates. But sadly, those debates too often distract from the much greater crime—how our financial and political elites, with the support of the all-powerful Federal Reserve, neutralized meaningful regulatory oversight and left us to fend for ourselves. Ferguson asserts, "There needs to be a renewal of American faith in the founding principles. A lot of ordinary Americans, especially businessmen, yearn for this and resent the crony capitalism they see between Washington and Wall Street."[5]

Despite our shortcomings, we remain a government of the people, for the people, and by the people. As such, we are called to act. We are compelled to work tirelessly to reassert the constitutional principles established by our forefathers so that future generations might have a real shot at the American dream.

And there is hope. Wall Street, when well run, is the embodiment of the American spirit, providing the fuel and inspiration for new products, new companies, and new ideas that revolutionize our nation and the world. To improve the general welfare of our people, we need free and fair markets along with vigorous competition. Our nation needs to reengage capitalism so that credit flows, families prosper, businesses thrive, and risk takers blaze new trails of opportunity. In order to recover the American spirit, we need to expose the real truths of this crisis conveniently left uncovered by the media and politicians and also to put forth strong public policy recommendations.

Some folks are so disillusioned with the damage of the past few years that they're ready to declare anarchy, while others would seemingly embrace socialism. But I caution people on both ends of the spectrum not to take the material presented herein and bend it to fit your personal politics. While America has always had its share of ideologues, our strength has always come from finding and embracing the truth and building a consensus upon it. The truth does not align itself with any individual interest groups or political parties. It may at times be subject to review or difference of opinion, but ultimately, most people who care about the truth will know it when they see it. The key question is, how can we ensure the truth reaches the public against the wishes and will of those who work tirelessly to impede it?

Certainly many regulators, governmental overseers, and financial executives—especially Wall Street CEOs—will have little interest in the truths laid bare and the reforms I propose. These proposals are intended to open the doors and windows of Wall Street's self-regulatory organizations and other entities so that global investors and consumers, and American taxpayers, can get an unvarnished look not only at our regulators but also at Wall Street itself.

With regulatory transparency, we will learn how Wall Street was able to engineer the manipulation of Libor and other overnight interest rates, mortgage fraud, naked short selling, insider trading activities, front running via high-frequency trading on our equity exchanges, money laundering, and so much more. More substantial reforms, though, are needed to fumigate FINRA and the SEC, and simultaneously implement meaningful investor protections. I readily acknowledge that the reforms and public policy proposals detailed below are far from comprehensive, but given Washington's gridlock and basic disinterest in addressing these issues, I submit that even these broad strokes are badly needed in our public debate. To that end, I offer the following recommended reforms and public policy proposals.

FINANCIAL REGULATORY REFORMS

1. **The SEC and FINRA should mandate an outline of risk parameters.**   Written in plain English, this risk assessment vehicle should be delivered to each and every retail investor prior to every transaction. It should also be available to institutional investors upon request. Included in this delivery should be a comprehensive listing of all fees, costs, expenses, loads, and charges, however defined.

2. **FINRA should release all details pertaining to its ARS liquidation.**   Tens of billions of dollars of ARS remain outstanding more than five full years after the ARS market collapsed. The public deserves to know all the details relating to FINRA's liquidation of its ARS holdings in 2007. Did FINRA engage in a form of front running or insider trading? These details, when released, will shed real light on the manner in which this self-regulatory organization operates.

3. **All ARS holders should be made whole.**   Given the liquidity in the marketplace, any entities that have not yet redeemed their ARS holders should be required to do so immediately. Wall Street's greatest fraud has run long enough. After more than five years, companies should end the pain that continues to strangle thousands of investors. Companies should utilize existing cash holdings or issue debt or equity to make these investors whole in what were supposed to be cash-alternative investments.

4. **Wall Street arbitration should be optional, not mandatory.**   Investors or employees on Wall Street who would like to pursue justice through the legal system should have that option. Additionally, the results of arbitration and legal

cases should be matters of public record so that bad behaviors and the adjudication thereof may serve as a precedent and inhibit the perpetuation of the same behaviors in the future. The days of Wall Street's kangaroo court need to end. Interestingly enough, in mid-2013, an SEC executive Luis Aguilar broke ranks and put forth a similar proposal.[6]

5. **FINRA should be subject to an independent outside audit and the Freedom of Information Act.**   This audit should be undertaken by an independent outside entity, report to a newly devised Financial Regulatory Review Board (more details on this in a moment), and include annual reviews of all FINRA finances and investment activities far in excess of what is done currently. Given that FINRA utilizes the absolute immunity privilege to defend itself, it should most definitely be subject to respond to Freedom of Information Act requests. Transparency remains the great disinfectant.

6. **Private financial self-regulatory organizations should no longer have absolute immunity.**   While I strongly believe that the very practice of self-regulation within the financial industry should end, the practice of employing absolute immunity as a defense should unquestionably cease. Absolute immunity without full and total transparency is simply a license to steal. Self-regulators should not be subjected to trivial lawsuits, but they should not be allowed to hide under the cloak of absolute immunity either. I propose a privately run Financial Regulatory Review Board to determine which cases brought against a self-regulatory organization should be recommended to proceed to trial for adjudication by the courts.

7. **Congress should compel FINRA to address the questions raised in the Amerivet, Standard Investment Chartered,**

and Benchmark Financial cases. Given that FINRA should not be allowed to hide under a cover of absolute immunity, FINRA should be mandated to address the questions raised in the Amerivet, Standard Investment Chartered, and Benchmark Financial cases under the auspices of an independent investigator. Did officials lie verbally and in writing in the merger that formed FINRA? Was $178 to $387 million misappropriated in that process? What was the true nature of the relationship between Bernie Madoff and FINRA? Did FINRA utilize material nonpublic information in order to liquidate its ARS holdings in 2007? So many great questions. So few real answers (yet).

8. **Congress needs to pass—and the president needs to sign— HR 757.** This piece of legislation, sponsored by Representative Scott Garrett (R-NJ), will reform the Securities Investor Protection Corporation so that investors in our nation will never again be compromised by the sham investor protection perpetrated by Wall Street and SIPC. The Wall Street lobby worked hard to sidetrack this reform. In late 2012, it was referred to committee.

9. **Congress should authorize and launch a privately run Office of Whistleblower Protection.** In conjunction with a Financial Regulatory Review Board, I also propose the launching of an Office of Whistleblower Protection. While the newly launched Dodd-Frank legislation includes a whistleblower program, learning that the SEC's enforcement division is likely to share information provided by whistleblowers back to the firms allegedly violating the law is a serious disincentive for whistleblowers to come forward. As such, whistleblowers should be able to bring their

information to a separate Office of Whistleblower Protection with total confidence that their identities will be protected and their allegations fully vetted and pursued. This office could serve as a model for similar initiatives within other areas of the government as well.

I would also propose that the Office of Whistleblower Protection in conjunction with the Financial Regulatory Review Board be charged with monitoring the revolving door between Wall Street and Washington so that abuses and conflicts of interest are mitigated. Lawyers should not be allowed to directly intervene with SEC personnel in the manner that Mary Jo White allegedly did on behalf of Morgan Stanley.

10. **Congress should hold a public hearing and address the points raised by the Project on Government Oversight.**   Congress is long overdue to address this detailed letter presented by POGO in regard to FINRA.

PUBLIC POLICY PROPOSALS

These public policy proposals are intended to address significant gaps in our country's political and economic foundations, and promote the ethical practice of free market capitalism.

1. Financial self-regulation does not work.

FINRA and the other financial self-regulatory organizations should cease to exist, as it is impossible to reconcile the interests of their two masters. To think that Goldman Sachs, J.P. Morgan, Morgan Stanley, Bank of America, Citigroup, Wells Fargo, and every other bank can fund a regulator that will, in turn, aggressively oversee their activities is simply ridiculous.

Recall that FINRA has levied an annual average of $50 million in fines since its inception in 2007, while our economy has lost $12.8 trillion in value due to the crisis emanating from Wall Street. FINRA's parent, the NASD, was founded in 1939 upon the premise that an industry-funded self-regulatory organization would save the government money. How has that premise worked over the course of the last five-plus years?

I am not so naive to think that we can merely scrap self-regulation and fold the efforts into government oversight via the SEC. Neither the SEC nor their overseers atop Capitol Hill have displayed sufficient competence or courage to regulate Wall Street effectively. I recommend that our current financial self-regulatory organizations be incorporated into the SEC only in concert with the oversight of a Financial Regulatory Review Board populated by a coterie of qualified and experienced financial statesmen.

2. Financial Regulatory Review Board

Many cities throughout America have incorporated private, independent police review boards to address a host of issues and abuses that have transpired within their police departments. In similar fashion, I believe strongly that Congress should authorize the launch of a Financial Regulatory Review Board staffed and run by highly qualified private individuals with a passion for public service.

The SEC and others atop Capitol Hill, throughout Washington, and on Wall Street will assuredly maintain that there is no need for such an aggressive move as this. In fact, Washington insiders would likely maintain that a newly launched Dodd-Frank initiative designated as the Financial Stability Oversight Council (FSOC) would address my point. A quick review of the FSOC exposes the fact that those sitting on this council come from within the currently captured—if not corrupted—regulatory oversight system. Even former FDIC chair Sheila Bair weighed in on the ineffectiveness of the FSOC: "The ability of the council to function is also compromised by the fact that it is headed by an administration cabinet member. That sets up an inherent conflict with his FSOC responsibilities to promote a safe, stable financial system, even if it conflicts with administration policies or rubs powerful political constituencies the wrong way."[7]

Additionally, insiders will also opine that Dodd-Frank is directed to launch an Office of the Investor Advocate. However, none other than SEC commissioner Luis Aguilar informs us, "As of today, almost three years after Dodd-Frank became law, the Commission still has not created the Office of the Investor Advocate." Juxtapose that failure to perform on the part of the SEC next to "the results of a recent survey reported in March 2013 show[ing] that, by an overwhelming margin, 84 percent of Americans want the federal government to play an active role in protecting investors."[8]

There is no shortage of leaders who could be enticed to serve the public interest in overseeing the management of a revised SEC that also encompasses all other self-regulatory organizations. Reporting lines would run from the SEC to the review board and from the review board to Congress. Pay these private citizens engaged in public service commensurate with their talents and expertise, knowing full well that an ounce of prevention beats a pound of cure. Make these positions full time, with a term of three years, to build continuity. I believe the following individuals would be more than qualified to sit on this review board and provide apolitical oversight of the markets and related regulatory affairs. They may not be well received by current regulators, Congress, or the industry, but that only further confirms their value:

- **Gary Aguirre:** lawyer without peer in understanding the inner workings of the SEC and fighting for real justice on behalf of investors and the American public.

- **Sheila Bair:** nineteenth chairperson of the Federal Deposit Insurance Corporation. Bair has displayed not only a keen understanding of our financial system but also possesses a real appreciation that cronyism has no place in a free market capitalist system.

- **Neil Barofsky:** special inspector general of the Troubled Asset Relief Program (TARP). Barofsky is also a successful former prosecutor of international drug kingpins and white-collar crime.

- **Amar Bhide:** Thomas Schmidheiny Professor at the Tufts University Fletcher School of Law and Diplomacy. Bhide has real-world experience on Wall Street along with extensive insights from studying innovation and entrepreneurship. A founding member of the Center on Capitalism and Society, Bhide has authored several publications on strategy, finance, and firm governance.

- **William Black:** lawyer, author, academic, and former bank regulator with expertise in white-collar crime, public finance, and financial regulation. Black is highly regarded for having developed the concept of control fraud.

- **Richard Bowen:** the "canary in the coal mine" at Citigroup who had warned Robert Rubin and others of the systemic fraud within Citi's mortgage operations. Bowen has 35 years of experience in credit, finance, and information technology.

- **Richard Greenfield:** lawyer with over 30 years of experience in banking, securities, and consumer litigation. Greenfield also was a lawyer for Amerivet Securities, Standard

Investment Chartered, and Benchmark Financial in their
suits brought against FINRA.

- **Bill Isaac:** former chair of the FDIC, which he joined at
  the tender age of 34 in 1978 and then headed from 1981
  through 1985, a period of tremendous unrest in our nation's
  banking history. Isaac has also founded and managed financial consulting firms, having previously practiced general
  corporate law with a specialty in banking and antitrust law.
- **Simon Johnson:** former chief economist of the International
  Monetary Fund and current professor of entrepreneurship
  at the MIT Sloan School of Management. Johnson is also
  a senior fellow at the Peterson Institute for International
  Economics, a member of the Congressional Budget Office's
  Panel of Economic Advisors, and a member of the FDIC's
  Systemic Resolution Advisory Committee.
- **Harry Markopolos:** noted whistleblower who unearthed the
  scam perpetrated by Bernie Madoff and brought it to the
  SEC. He is a former investment portfolio manager who now
  pursues fraud investigations against Fortune 500 companies
  in the financial services and health-care industries.
- **David Skeel:** the S. Samuel Arsht Professor of Corporate
  Law at the University of Pennsylvania. Skeel has authored
  *The New Financial Deal: Understanding the Dodd-Frank Act
  and Its (Unintended) Consequences* and *Debt's Dominion: A
  History of Bankruptcy Law in America,* among other works.
  A strong proponent of promoting and protecting the rule
  of law.
- **Robert Wilmers:** current chairman and CEO of M&T
  Bank and a fierce advocate for strong and safe retail bank-
  ing. Wilmers has served on numerous banking councils and

was also a past director of the Federal Reserve Bank of New York.

3. Campaign Finance Reform

Central to the issues that led to our crisis is the endless flow of money from our major financial institutions—and other entities, including major trade unions—to the coffers of the perpetual campaigns being run in Washington. When did public service become a for-profit undertaking? Our electoral system is rapidly taking on the glow of a banana republic. If we want to prevent future crises, we need legislators in Congress and in state and federal executive offices who are not compromised by major checks from large corporate and union concerns. In order to accomplish this worthy goal, we need to enact the following:

a. A constitutional amendment overturning *Citizens United v. Federal Election Commission.*

   After this controversial ruling by the Supreme Court in 2010, numerous grassroots movements embraced the mantra that "money is not speech and that human beings, not corporations, are the only 'persons' entitled to constitutional rights."[9]

b. Embrace and implement proposals put forth by Harvard professor Lawrence Lessig, who envisions elections funded by a mix of public and limited private donations:

   Give every voter a $50 campaign voucher. The $50 comes from the tax pool. It can be given to any candidate who accepts only money from the vouchers (and maybe a limit of an optional voluntary $100 per single voter). Thus all campaign money would come in very small amounts from The People.

Lessig calculates that the total amount of money raised this public way would be three times the amount raised by private means in the last election cycles, and therefore more than adequate. But it would break the grip of corporate influence over what is voted up. The result would not be harmonious utopia, but [rather] the usual give-and-take compromises of politics—which the US has not seen in decades. The issues that people cared about would return to the agenda.[10]

4. End "Too Big To Fail"

We all know Wall Street banks that are too big to fail, regulate, or prosecute are too big to exist. We cannot presume that those who benefit from a "too big to fail" model will ever work toward ending it. We need to restructure the Wall Street oligopoly if we ever hope to return to true, free market capitalism. How might we unwind an oligopolistic banking system that accrues a projected $83 billion taxpayer subsidy on an annual basis? (That $83 billion is the equivalent of 3 cents on every tax dollar collected.)

Reinstituting the Glass-Steagall Act—which separates commercial banking entities and their federally insured deposits from investment banking activities including trading and proprietary activities—would be ideal. The splitting up of our "too big to fail" banks in conjunction with implementing rigorous capital ratios and practicing meaningful regulatory oversight would allow the principles and long-term benefits of free market capitalism to once again reign.

Regrettably, given the current enormity of these institutions, that ideal is not practical. So I propose a plan B. Start by ring-fencing those activities within banks that should not be afforded any sort of government support, including: fixed income, equity, and derivatives sales and trading; proprietary investments; private banking investment and wealth management; prime brokerage; and asset management. The European Union commissioned an expert group to study this situation within its economic sphere and made this same recommendation via a paper designated the Liikanen Report.[11]

Establish a timetable leading to a firm date when there is no chance of a government bailout, so that clients engaging banks within these realms fully understand that they are taking the credit risk of that specific organization when entering into a transaction. The key to this process is enabling regulators and government officials to get their arms around the derivatives exposures already on the banks' books. Given the size of the derivatives market and circuitous nature of credit exposures, transitioning these books of business so that market participants understand that the government will not be there to bail them out will be a big challenge. But it's certainly not impossible. Within the other market segments, the transition from the "too big to fail" model should be relatively simple.

Naturally, the banks will fight this process tooth and nail because they will lose the enormous subsidy that accrues to them under the current model. They will argue that the flow of credit to the economy will be impinged by such a market-based approach. The same fictitious argument was presented by Freddie Mac and Fannie Mae when reformists in Washington tried to curtail their efforts. The failure of those initiatives led to front door and backdoor bailouts in the hundreds of billions of dollars. The banks will also threaten to move business units, especially their derivatives businesses, to other regions, most likely Europe; however, the EU is further along in advancing a financial regulatory rigor as evidenced by the written, but not yet implemented, Liikanen Report. Without a true market mechanism to impose discipline on the banks, they will always be predisposed to maximize social risk for personal gain—in other words, "Heads we win, tails you lose."

Once we've ring-fenced the investment banking activities and employed rigorous regulatory oversight, we must push to formalize the separation of business activities of the investment banks and commercial banks. This actual splitting up of the major banks will eliminate the chance that bank management might somehow use sleight of hand to redirect consumer deposits from their commercial enterprises to their investment banking operations.

With meaningful movement on these reforms and proposals, we can send the strongest message yet of real advocacy to all investors, consumers, and taxpayers. To do that, though, we not only need to have our regulators, politicians, and bankers in separate beds, but also separate rooms. In the process, we can begin to aerate the regulatory system, exorcise the cronyism, and derail the oligopoly. The badly needed fresh air will energize our economy, promote real competition in the marketplace, and reassert the premise of true free market capitalism as the engine for better days ahead.

Future generations deserve nothing less.

God bless America.

NOTES

CHAPTER 1: PILLOW TALK

1. Randall Smith, Tom McGinty, and Kara Scannell, "Obama's Pick to Head SEC Has Record of Being a Regulator with a Light Touch," *Wall Street Journal*, January 15, 2009, http://online.wsj.com/article/SB123194123553080959.html.
2. "About FINRA" and "More About FINRA," *Financial Industry Regulatory Authority*, accessed July 16, 2013, http://www.finra.org/AboutFINRA/.
3. "2007 Year in Review and Annual Financial Report: Shaping the Future of Regulation," *Financial Industry Regulatory Authority*, accessed September 4, 2013, http://www.finra.org/web/groups/corporate/@corp/@about/@ar/documents/corporate/p038602.pdf.
4. Testimony of Harry Markopolos before the U.S. House of Representatives Committee on Financial Services, February 4, 2009, http://online.wsj.com/public/resources/documents/MarkopolosTestimony20090203.pdf; John Churchill, "SEC, FINRA Hit Hard by Markopolos Testimony," *Wealth Management.com*, February 4, 2009, accessed September 24, 2013, http://wealthmanagement.com/regulationsec-finra-hit-hard-markopolos-testimony.
5. "U.S. Capital Markets Competitiveness: The Unfinished Agenda," *United States Chamber of Commerce*, Summer 2011, https://www.uschamber.com/sites/default/files/reports/1107_UnfinishedAgenda_WEB.pdf.

CHAPTER 2: THE MONEY TRAIL

1. "Annual Report of the Federal Trade Commission for the Fiscal Year Ended June 30, 1933," *Federal Trade Commission*, accessed August, 28, 2013, http://www.ftc.gov/os/annualreports/ar1933.pdf.
2. Larry Bumgardner, "A Brief History of the 1930s Securities Laws in the United States—And the Potential Lesson for Today," *The Journal of Global Business Management*, 4, accessed September 4, 2013, http://www.jgbm.org/page/5%20Larry%20Bumgardner.pdf.
3. Securities Exchange Act of 1934, 15 U.S.C. § 78a, *US Securities and Exchange Commission*, 1934, http://www.sec.gov/about/laws/sea34.pdf.
4. SEC Rule 10b-5, 17 C.F.R. 240.10b-5 amendment to the Securities Exchange Act of 1934, 1942, http://www.gpo.gov/fdsys/pkg/CFR-2011-title17-vol3/pdf/CFR-2011-title17-vol3-sec240-10b-5.pdf.

5. A Discussion of the Maloney Act Program by George C. Mathews, Commissioner, Securities and Exchange Commission, *US Securities and Exchange Commission*, http://www.sec.gov/news/speech/1938/102338mathews.pdf.

6. Tamar Hed-Hofmann, "The Maloney Act Experiment," *Boston College Law Review*, 1965, 187, http://lawdigitalcommons.bc.edu/bclr/vol6/iss2/3.

7. Ibid.

8. Francis A. Bonner, "The Over-the-Counter Market and The Maloney Act," speech delivered before the Annual Convention of the Investment Bankers Association of America, 1938, https://www.sec.gov/news/speech/1938/102338bonner.pdf.

9. Hed-Hoffman, "The Maloney Act Experiment," 208.

10. Ibid., 194.

11. Ibid., 217, 211.

12. Ibid., 212.

13. "NASD History," *Funding Universe*, accessed August 28, 2013, http://www.fundinguniverse.com/company-histories/nasd-history/.

14. Robert G. Kaiser, *So Damn Much Money*, New York: Alfred A. Knopf, 2009, 23.

15. John W. Dean, "Passing Bills: A Journalist Investigates How Lobbyists Cash in on Congressional Influence," *Boston Globe*, February 15, 2009, www.boston.com/ae/books/articles/2009/02/15/passing_bills/?page=full.

16. "Public Broadcasting System," *Bill Moyers Journal*, February 13, 2009, http://www.pbs.org/moyers/journal/02132009/watch.html.

17. Michelle Hirsch, "New Insider Trading Law Winks at Some Violators," *Fiscal Times*, March 23, 2012, accessed September 4, 2013, http://www.thefiscaltimes.com/Articles/2012/03/23/New-Insider-Trading-Law-Winks-at-Some-Violations.aspx#page1.

18. *Skilling v. United States*, 561 U.S., Supreme Court of the United States, October 2009, http://www.supremecourt.gov/opinions/09pdf/08-1394.pdf.

19. Hirsch, "New Insider Trading Law."

20. Robert Weissman and James Donahue, "Sold Out: How Wall Street and Washington Betrayed America," *Wall Street Watch*, March 2009, http://www.wallstreetwatch.org/reports/sold_out.pdf.

21. Ibid.

CHAPTER 3: COPS ON THE TAKE

1. "2007 Year in Review and Annual Financial Report: Letter from the CEO," *Financial Industry Regulatory Authority*, accessed September 4, 2013, http://apps.finra.org/annual_report/2007/ar07.html.

2. Ibid.

3. Barack Obama, "2009 Inaugural Address," Washington, DC, January 20, 2009, www.whitehouse.gov/blog/inaugural-address.

4. Barack Obama, "Memorandum for the Heads of Executive Departments and Agencies: Transparency and Open Government," Washington, DC, January 21, 2009, http://www.whitehouse.gov/the_press_office/TransparencyandOpenGovernment.

5. Donna Mitchell, "FINRA Rebuffs Amerivet's Demand to Inspect Records," *The Compliance Exchange*, August 27, 2009, http://compliancex.com/finra-rebuffs-amerivets-demand-to-inspect-records/.

6. "2007 Year in Review," *Financial Industry Regulatory Authority*, accessed September 4, 2013, http://apps.finra.org/annual_report/2007/ar07.html.

7. Testimony of Harry Markopolos Before the U.S. House of Representatives Committee on Financial Services, February 4, 2009, http://online.wsj.com /public/resources/documents/MarkopolosTestimony20090203.pdf.

8. Harry Markopolos, "Riveting Testimony from a Great American," *Sense on Cents*, February 4, 2009, http://www.senseoncents.com/2009/02/riveting -testimony-from-a-great-american-harry-markopolos/.

9. Markopolos, "Riveting Testimony"; John Churchill, "SEC, FINRA Hit Hard by Markopolos Testimony," *WealthManagement.com*, February 4, 2009, accessed September 24, 2013, http://wealthmanagement.com/regulation /sec-finra-hit-hard-markopolos-testimony.

10. Darrell Preston, "FINRA Oversees Auction-Rate Arbitrations After Exit," *Bloomberg*, April 29, 2009, http://www.bloomberg.com/apps/news?pid= newsarchive&sid=agMSn6dueL3I.

CHAPTER 4: OUT IN THE COLD

1. *Bear, Stearns & Co. et al. before the Securities and Exchange Commission*, file No 3-12310, May 31, 2006, http://www.sec.gov/litigation/admin/2006/33 -8684.pdf.

2. "NASD 2004 Annual Financial Report," *National Association of Securities Dealers* (2004), accessed September 4, 2013, http://www.finra.org/web /groups/corporate/@corp/@about/@ar/documents/corporate/p014280 .pdf.

3. Darrel Preston, "FINRA Oversees Auction-Rate Arbitrations After Exit," *Bloomberg*, April 29, 2009, http://www.bloomberg.com/apps/news?pid= newsarchive&sid=agMSn6dueL3I.

4. Ibid.

5. Ed Dowling, "FINRA and Auction Rate Securities," *Sense on Cents*, May 3, 2009, http://www.senseoncents.com/2009/05/ars-investor-makes-public -plea/.

6. Preston, "FINRA Oversees Auction-Rate Arbitrations After Exit."

7. Mary L. Schapiro, "The Road Ahead in Regulation," Ethics and Leadership Lecture at Dominican University, River Forest, Illinois, October 14, 2008, http://www.finra.org/Newsroom/Speeches/Schapiro/P117298.

8. Preston, "FINRA Oversees Auction-Rate Arbitrations After Exit."

9. "Partial Redemption of Auction Rate Securities: FINRA Issues Guidance to Broker-Dealers on Partial Redemptions of Auction Rate Securities," Regulatory Notice 08-2, Financial Industry Regulatory Authority, April 2008, http://www.finra.org/Industry/Regulation/Notices/2008/P038406.

10. Daisy Maxey, "For Many Auction-Rate Investors, the Freeze Goes On," *Wall Street Journal*, March 13, 2012, online.wsj.com/article/SB100014240529702 03960804577243554110930094.html.

11. Marsha, "Auction Rate Comments Reflect Real Pain," *Sense on Cents*, April 21, 2011, http://www.senseoncents.com/2011/04/auction-rate-comments -reflect-real-pain/.

12. Kathy, "Auction Rate Comments Reflect Real Pain," *Sense on Cents*, April 21, 2011, http://www.senseoncents.com/2011/04/auction-rate-comments -reflect-real-pain/.

13. JoanZ, "Auction Rate Comments Reflect Real Pain," *Sense on Cents*, April 21, 2011, http://www.senseoncents.com/2011/04/auction-rate-comments-reflect-real-pain/.

14. Susie, "Auction Rate Comments Reflect Real Pain," *Sense on Cents*, April 21, 2011, http://www.senseoncents.com/2011/04/auction-rate-comments-reflect-real-pain/.

15. Wink, "Auction Rate Comments Reflect Real Pain," *Sense on Cents*, April 21, 2011, http://www.senseoncents.com/2011/04/auction-rate-comments-reflect-real-pain/; Oppenheimer & Co. entered into a settlement of a lawsuit brought by Massachusetts and a related lawsuit in New York that required the company to repurchase the ARS bonds from investors. http://www.boston.com/business/ticker/2010/02/oppenheimer_set.html. However, according to reports, they were only required to buy back $25,000 per account in New York and there were limits to the amounts they were required to buy back in Massachusetts as well. Ibid. This likely accounts for the ongoing bitterness expressed in this and some of the following posts.

16. Dave, "ARS Update: Jefferson County, Oppenheimer Holdings," *Sense on Cents*, November 15, 2011, http://www.senseoncents.com/2011/11/ars-update-jefferson-county-oppenheimer/.

17. Ibid.

CHAPTER 5: KANGAROO COURT

1. Edward S. O'Neal and Daniel R. Solin, "Mandatory Arbitration of Securities Disputes: A Statistical Analysis of How Claimants Fare," *Securities Litigation and Consulting Group*, accessed September 4, 2013, http://www.slcg.com/pdf/workingpapers/Mandatory%20Arbitration%20Study.pdf.

2. "Dispute Resolution Statistics," *Financial Industry Regulatory Authority*, accessed December 3, 2012 and September 4, 2013, http://www.finra.org/ArbitrationAndMediation/FINRADisputeResolution/AdditionalResources/Statistics/.

3. Dan Fitzpatrick, "Didn't See Risk, and Got Stung," *Wall Street Journal*, June 11, 2010, http://online.wsj.com/article/SB10001424052748703627704575299111742983330.html.

4. Testimony of William Francis Galvin before the US House Subcommittee on Capital Markets, Insurance, and Government Sponsored Enterprises, "A Review of the Securities Arbitration System," March 17, 2005, http://financialservices.house.gov/media/pdf/031705wfg.pdf.

5. "Code of Arbitration," *National Association of Securities Dealers*, accessed September 4, 2013, http://www.finra.org/web/groups/arbitrationmediation/@arbmed/@arbion/documents/arbmed/p018653.pdf; Edward S. O'Neal and Daniel R. Solin, "Mandatory Arbitration of Securities Disputes: A Statistical Analysis of How Claimants Fare," *Securities Litigation and Consulting Group*, accessed September 4, 2013, http://www.slcg.com/pdf/workingpapers/Mandatory%20Arbitration%20Study.pdf.

6. "FINRA Proposes to Permanently Give Investors the Option of All-Public Arbitration Panels," *Financial Industry Regulatory Authority*, September 28, 2010, http://www.finra.org/Newsroom/NewsReleases/2010/P122178.

7. "Arbitration Myths," *The Guilliano Law Firm, P.C.*, accessed September 4, 2013, http://www.stockbrokerfraud.com/securities-arbitration/arbitration-myths.

8. Bill Cohan, "Wall Street's Captive Arbitrators Strike Again," *Bloomberg*, July 8, 2012, http://www.bloomberg.com/news/2012-07-08/wall-street-s-captive-arbitrators-strike-again.html.

9. Bill Cohan, "Wall Street's Kangaroo Court Gets a Black Eye," *Bloomberg*, July 29, 2012, http://www.bloomberg.com/news/2012-07-29/wall-street-s-kangaroo-court-gets-a-black-eye.html.

10. Al Lewis, "Broker Bankrupted in Kangaroo Court," *Market Watch*, March 14, 2012, http://articles.marketwatch.com/2012-03-14/commentary/3116 3067_1_finra-financial-industry-regulatory-authority-morgan-stanley.

11. Rule 12606: Record of Proceedings, adopted by SR-NASD-2003-158, eff. April 16, 2007, amended by SR-FINRA-2008-021, eff. Dec. 15, 2008, Financial Industry Regulatory Authority, http://finra.complinet.com/en/display/display.html?rbid=2403&element_id=4176.

12. *Morgan Stanley Smith Barney LLC, vs Mark D. Mensack vs Morgan Stanley & Co., Inc., Peter Prunty and Rich Maratea*, Dispute Resolution Arbitration Case Number 10-1687, Financial Industry Regulatory Authority, January 13, 2012, http://pogoarchives.org/m/fo/finra-response-20120113.pdf.

CHAPTER 6: INCEST

1. Iren Levina, James Crotty, and Gerald Epstein, "Ending Too Big To Fail: Facts and Figures on Size and Concentration of U.S. Commercial and Investment Banks," *A Committee of Economists and other Experts for Stable, Accountable, Fair and Efficient Financial Reform*, Political Economy Research Institute, April 26, 2010, http://www.peri.umass.edu/fileadmin/pdf/other_publication_types/SAFERbriefs/SAFER_issue_brief22.pdf.

2. Eric Rasmussen, "Swimming in Shallow Water," *Financial Advisor*, March 30, 2012, http://www.fa-mag.com/news/swimming-in-shallow-water-101 78.html.

3. "2012 FINRA District Committee Election Candidate Profiles – District 10: Small Firm Representative Candidate," *Financial Industry Regulatory Authority*, accessed September 4, 2013, http://www.finra.org/Industry/District/P188062.

4. *Amerivet Securities v. Financial Industry Regulatory Authority*, Superior Court of the District of Columbia, August 10, 2009, 2-5: 6-16, http://www.senseoncents.com/wp-content/uploads/2009/08/amerivet-vs-finra.pdf.

5. Sophie Gilbert, "Who Are the Wealthiest Members of the Obama Administration?" *Washingtonian*, March 27, 2009, http://www.washingtonian.com/blogs/capitalcomment/1600-pennsylvania-avenue/who-are-the-wealthiest-members-of-the-obama-administration.php.

6. *Amerivet Securities v. FINRA*, 8: 24.

7. Ibid., 9: 27.

8. *America's Nightly Scoreboard*, Fox Business, September 3, 2009, http://www.senseoncents.com/2009/09/attorney-claims-wall-streets-cop-finra-invested-in-madoff/; http://www.senseoncents.com/2009/09/attorney-representing-amerivet-securities-makes-claim-finra-insider-confirms-investment-in-madoff/.

9. "Report of the 2009 Special Review Committee on FINRA's Examination Program in Light of the Stanford and Madoff Schemes," *Financial Industry Regulatory Authority*, September 2009, http://www.finra.org/web/groups/corporate/@corp/documents/corporate/p120078.pdf.

10. Elton Johnson, Jr., "Truth, Transparency, and Accountability Initiative Campaign," *Amerivet Securities Inc.*, 2011, accessed September 4, 2013, http://amerivetsecurities.com/about-us/executive-bios/elton-johnson-jr/truth-transparency-and-accountability-initiative-ttai.

11. Ibid.

12. Donna Mitchell, "FINRA Rebuffs Amerivet's Demand to Inspect Records," *The Compliance Exchange,* August 27, 2009, http://compliancex.com/finra-rebuffs-amerivets-demand-to-inspect-records/.

13. *America's Nightly Scoreboard,* Fox Business, September 3, 2009, http://www.senseoncents.com/2009/09/attorney-claims-wall-streets-cop-finra-invested-in-madoff/.

CHAPTER 7: IMMUNITY

1. "Stern: Bet Probe 'Worst Situation that I Have Ever Experienced,'" *ESPN,* July 25, 2007, http://sports.espn.go.com/nba/news/story?id=2947237.

2. "Cuneo Gilbert Out to Disinfect FINRA with Some Sunlight," *Corporate Crime Reporter,* September 17, 2009, accessed September 4, 2013, http://www.corporatecrimereporter.com/finra091709.htm.

3. "FINRA: NASD and NYSE Member Regulation Combine to Form the Financial Industry Regulatory Authority," *Financial Industry Regulatory Authority,* July 30, 2007, http://www.finra.org/Newsroom/NewsReleases/2007/p036329.

4. "Cuneo Gilbert Out to Disinfect FINRA."

5. "NASD 2006 Year in Review and Annual Financial Report," *National Association of Securities Dealers,* accessed September 4, 2013, http://apps.finra.org/annual_report/2006/ar06.html.

6. Larry Doyle, "Mary Schapiro Has Some 'Splainin To Do," *Sense on Cents,* October 8, 2009, http://www.senseoncents.com/2009/10/mary-schapiro-has-some-splainin-to-do/.

7. *Standard Investment Chartered Inc. v. Financial Industry Regulatory Authority,* United States District Court, Southern District of New York, filed October 20, 2009, http://www.senseoncents.com/wp-content/uploads/2009/10/REDACTED_File_Stamped_Standard_SAC.pdf.

8. Ibid.

9. Susan Antilla and Jesse Westbrook, "Brokers' Lawyer Says FINRA Understated Merger Payment," *Bloomberg,* December 17, 2009, http://www.bloomberg.com/news/2009-12-17/brokers-lawyer-says-finra-understated-merger-payment-update1-.html.

10. *Standard Investment Chartered Inc. v. Financial Industry Regulatory Authority*; Larry Doyle, "Mary Schapiro Has Some 'Splainin To Do," *Sense on Cents.*

11. Ibid.

12. Ibid.

13. Ibid.

14. Ibid.

15. *Benchmark Financial Services Inc. v. Financial Industry Regulatory Authority,* United States District Court, Southern District of New York, filed December 23, 2008, accessed September 4, 2013, http://www.corporatecrimereporter.com/documents/benchmark.pdf; *Standard Investment Chartered Inc. v. Financial Industry Regulatory Authority,* United States District Court, Southern District of New York, filed October 20, 2009, http://www.senseoncents

.com/wp-content/uploads/2009/10/REDACTED_File_Stamped_Standar
d_SAC.pdf.

16. Larry Doyle, "Disenchanted FINRA Member Speaks Out," *Sense on Cents*, February 15, 2010, http://www.senseoncents.com/2010/02/disench anted-finra-member-speaks-out/.

17. Mary L. Schapiro, "Testimony Concerning the State of the Financial Crisis," remarks before the Financial Crisis Inquiry Commission, US Securities and Exchange Commission, January 14, 2010, http://www.sec.gov/news/testi mony/2010/ts011410mls.htm.

18. Dan Jamieson "Broker-Dealer Wants Supreme Court to Rule on FINRA Suit," *Investment News*, January 1, 2012, http://www.investmentnews.com /article/20120101/REG/301019975.

19. Larry Doyle's interview with Richard Greenfield, *Sense on Cents*, October 18, 2009, http://www.senseoncents.com/2009/10/no-quarter-radios-sense -on-cents-with-larry-doyle-welcomes-richard-greenfield-sunday-night-at -8pm-edt/.

20. Ibid.

21. "Declaration of F. Joseph Warin in Support of NASD Defendants' Motion For a Protective Order Preserving the Confidentiality of Documents," *Standard Investment Chartered Inc. v. Financial Industry Regulatory Authority*, United States District Court, Southern District of New York, January 14, 2010, http://www.senseoncents.com/wp-content/uploads/2013/09/Warin_ Declaration_ISO_Protective_Order-1.pdf.

CHAPTER 8: FAKE SECURITY

1. Franklin D. Roosevelt, "Transcript of Speech Regarding the Banking Crisis," *Federal Deposit Insurance Commission*, March 12, 1933, accessed September 4, 2013, http://www.fdic.gov/about/history/3-12-33transcript.html.

2. Securities Investor Protection Act, 15 U.S.C. §§ 78aaa et seq, US Congress, 1970, http://www.uscourts.gov/FederalCourts/Bankruptcy/BankruptcyBas ics/SIPA.aspx.

3. Ibid.

4. "The SIPC Mission," *Securities Investor Protection Corporation*, accessed September 4, 2013, http://www.sipc.org/Who/SIPCMission.aspx.

5. "2007 Annual Report," *Securities Investor Protection Corporation*, April 30, 2008, http://www.sipc.org/Portals/0/PDF/SIPC_2007_Annual_Report_ FINAL.pdf.

6. Hearing before the Subcommittee on Capital Markets, Insurance, and Government Sponsored Enterprises of the Committee on Financial Services, US House of Representatives, July 14, 2009, http://financialservices.house.gov /media/file/hearings/111/57.pdf; Bruce Carton, "SIPC Lacks Funds to Pay Madoff Victims," *Compliance Week*, August 1, 2009, 2013, http://www.com plianceweek.com/sipc-lacks-funds-to-pay-madoff-victims/article/188074/.

7. "Net Capital Rules Requirements for Brokers or Dealers: SEA Rule 15(c)3-1," *Financial Industry Regulatory Authority*, 2008, http://www.finra.org/web /groups/industry/@ip/@reg/@rules/documents/interpretationsfor/p0377 63.pdf.

8. "2008 Annual Report," *Securities Investor Protection Corporation*, April 30, 2009, http://www.sipc.org/Portals/0/PDF/SIPC%202008%20Annual%20 Report%20FINAL.pdf.

9. Ibid.

10. Ibid.

11. "Securities Investor Protection: Update on Matters Related to the Securities Investor Protection Corporation," *General Accounting Office*, August 11, 2003, http://www.gao.gov/assets/240/238921.html.

12. *Lisa Canavan, Leslie Goldsmith, and Judith Kalman on Behalf of Themselves and All Others Similarly Situated, Plaintiffs v. Stephen Harbeck, Armando J. Bucelo, Jr., Todd S. Farha, William H. Heyman, William S. Jasien, David G. Nason, Mark S. Shelton, and David J. Stockton, Defendants,* United States District Court, District of New Jersey, 57:175, http://clients.oakbridgeins.com/clients/blog/madofflawsuits/canavan.pdf.

13. Testimony by Paul E. Kanjorski, chairman, at committee hearing of House Committee on Financial Services, Subcommittee on Capital Markets, Insurance, and Government Sponsored Enterprises," Hearing on Securities Investor Protection Reform," December 9, 2009, http://www.senseoncents.com/wp-content/uploads/2009/12/TRANSCRIPT-12.09.091.pdf.

14. Ronnie Sue Ambrosino, "Madoff Victim Makes Impassioned Plea," *Sense on Cents*, August 12, 2009, http://www.senseoncents.com/2009/08/madoff-victim-makes-impassioned-plea/.

15. "New Times and First Ohio: Claims for Fictitious Securities," *Securities Investor Protection Corporation Modernization Task Force*, June 2010, http://www.sipcmodernization.org/Portals/0/New%20Times%20and%20First%20Ohio%20FINAL.pdf.

16. Testimony of Helen Davis Chaitman before the Subcommittee on Capital Markets, Insurance, and Government Sponsored Enterprises House Financial Services Committee, December 9, 2009, http://financialservices.house.gov/media/file/hearings/111/chaitman.pdf.

17. Larry Doyle, "America 2012: Justice for All? Really?," *Sense on Cents*, August 17, 2012, http://www.senseoncents.com/2012/08/america-2012-justice-for-all-really/.

CHAPTER 9: CODE OF SILENCE

1. "American Whistleblower Tour," *Government Accountability Project,* accessed September 4, 2013, http://www.whistleblower.org/action-center/american-whistleblower-tour; Larry Doyle, "Profiles in Courage Blowing the Whistle," *Sense on Cents,* February 22, 2012, http://www.senseoncents.com/2012/02/profiles-in-courage-blowing-the-whistle/.

2. "Not Much Bounty for SEC Whistleblower Program," *Project on Government Oversight,* April 5, 2010, http://pogoblog.typepad.com/pogo/2010/04/if-the-sec-has-a-whistleblower-program-but-nobody-ever-uses-it-does-it-really-exist.html.

3. Ibid.

4. Kara Scannell and Dan McCrum, "Emails Trace Trading of Stock Tips," *Financial Times,* January 18, 2012, http://www.ft.com/intl/cms/s/0/dc0fd158-4224-11e1-9506-00144feab49a.html#axzz1jwEHRKh0.

5. Testimony of Leyla M. Wydler to the U.S. Senate Banking Committee accessed September 4, 2013, http://www.banking.senate.gov/public/index.cfm?FuseAction=Files.View&FileStore_id=b4cf4d95-b043-4f84-ba47-603c4f90d4aa.

6. John Wasik, "Stanford's Ponzi Scam: The System Is Still Broken," *Forbes,* March 7, 2012, http://www.forbes.com/sites/johnwasik/2012/03/07/stanfords-ponzi-scam-the-system-is-still-broken/.

7. "Prosecuting Wall Street," *60 Minutes,* December 4, 2011, http://www.cbsnews.com/8301-18560_162-57336042/prosecuting-wall-street/.

8. Michael Richardson, "Putnam Investments Whistleblower Peter Scannell Described Beating in Congressional Testimony," *Examiner,* February 10, 2009, http://www.examiner.com/article/putnam-investments-whistleblower-peter-scannell-described-beating-congressional-testimony.

9. Ibid.

10. David Einhorn, "Fooling Some of the People All of the Time: A Long Short Story," *Fooling Some People.com,* accessed September 30, 2013, http://foolingsomepeople.com/main/message-from-david-qwhy-i-wrote-this-bookq.html.

11. John Crudele, "FINRA Whistleblower's Reward? He Gets Fired," *New York Post,* June 27, 2011, http://nypost.com/2011/06/28/finra-whistleblowers-reward-he-gets-fired/.

12. Ibid.

13. Ibid.

14. Zachary A. Goldfarb, "At SEC, The System Can Be Deaf to Whistleblowing," *Washington Post,* January 21, 2010, http://www.washingtonpost.com/wp-dyn/content/article/2010/01/20/AR2010012005125_2.html?sub=AR; see also William D. Cohan, "When Wall Street Watchdogs Hunt Whistle-Blowers," *Bloomberg,* August 19, 2012, http://www.bloomberg.com/news/2012-08-19/when-wall-street-watchdogs-hunt-whistle-blowers.html.

15. Referral of Report of Investigation: Case OIG-501 Disclosure of Nonpublic Information, US Securities and Exchange Commission, *Project on Government Oversight Archives,* March 30, 2009, 7, http://pogoarchives.org/m/er/sec-oig-report-20090330.pdf.

16. Ibid.

17. Michael Smallberg and Adam Zagorin, "Long Island Congressional Candidate Cited for Giving up JP Morgan Whistleblower," *Politics Daily,* January 28, 2010, http://www.politicsdaily.com/2010/01/28/long-island-congressional-candidate-cited-for-giving-up-jpmorgan/.

18. "Referral of Report of Investigation: Case OIG-501 Disclosure of Nonpublic Information," US Securities and Exchange Commission.

19. William D. Cohan, "When Wall Street Watchdogs Hunt Whistle-Blowers,"

20. Michael Smallberg and Adam Zagorin, "Long Island Congressional Candidate Cited for Giving up JP Morgan Whistleblower."

21. William J. Keniry, Letter to Peter Z. Sivere, September 23, 2011, accessed September 26, 2013, http://www.scribd.com/doc/72071871/Second-Dismissal.

22. George Demos' Answer to Complaint of Peter Sivere, State of New York Departmental Disciplinary Committee, Supreme Court, Appellate Division, First Judicial Department, https://docs.google.com/viewer?a=v&pid=sites&srcid=ZGVmYXVsdGRvbWFpbnx3aWxxaWFFta2VuaXJ5Y292ZXXJ1cHxneneDo3OGYwZDIwNzUxMWM5NjBk.

23. H. David Kotz, "Referral of Report of Investigation: Case OIG-501," United States Securities and Exchange Commission memo, March 30, 2009, https://docs.google.com/viewer?a=v&pid=sites&srcid=ZGVmYXVsdGRv

bWFpbnx3aWxsaWFta2VuXJ5Y292ZXJ1cHxneDoyNjBhNThlYmQ
yYTE3ZTJj.

24. "Aguirre Bio," Aguirre Law, APC., accessed September 4, 2013, http://
     aguirrelawapc.com/lawyer/Gary_Aguirre_cp3221.htm.

25. "SEC Settles with Aguirre," Government Accountability Project, June 29,
     2010, http://www.whistleblower.org/press/press-release-archive/2010/633-
     sec-settles-with-aguirre.

26. Gary Aguirre, "SEC/FOIA Debate, The Dodd-Frank Act: A FOIA Ex-
     emption for SEC Misconduct?" *Wall Street Lawyer*, volume 14, issue 9, Sep-
     tember 2010, http://aguirrelawapc.com/global_pictures/Attachment_5.pdf.

27. Matt Taibbi, "Why Isn't Wall Street in Jail?," *Rolling Stone*, February 16,
     2011, http://www.rollingstone.com/politics/news/why-isnt-wall-street-in-j
     ail-20110216.

28. Azam Ahmed and Ben Protess, "Pequot Insider Trading Case Drags On,"
     DealB%k, December 23, 2010, accessed September 7, 2013, dealbook.ny
     times.com/2010/12/23/pequot-insider-trading-case-drags-on/?_r=0;
     Thomas O. Gorman, "Lessons from the Pequot Investigation," *SEC Actions*,
     June 1, 2010, http://www.secactions.com/lessons-from-the-pequot-inves
     tigaton/.

29. "SEC Settles with Aguirre," *Government Accountability Project*, June 29,
     2010, accessed September 4, 2013, http://www.whistleblower.org/press
     /press-release-archive/2010/633-sec-settles-with-aguirre.

30. Ibid.

31. Ibid.

32. Ibid.

33. "The Firing of an SEC Attorney and the Investigation of Pequot Capital
     Management," US Senate, Committee on Finance, Committee on the Ju-
     diciary, *Project on Government Oversight Archives*, August 2007, http://
     pogoarchives.org/m/er/senate-pequot-report-august2007.pdf.

34. Letter from Gary J. Aguirre to Christopher Cox, Chairman, US Securi-
     ties and Exchange Commission, January 2, 2009, http://www.whistleblower
     .org/storage/documents/AguirreLetter.pdf.

35. "SEC Settles with Aguirre," Government Accountability Project.

36. Ibid.

37. David Scheer and Jesse Westbrook, "Pequot, Samberg Pay $28 Million to
     End Insider-Trading Probe," *Bloomberg*, May 27, 2010, http://www.bloom
     berg.com/news/2010-05-27/pequot-chief-samberg-to-pay-28-million-to
     -settle-sec-insider-trade-probe.html.

38. Letter from Gary J. Aguirre to Christopher Cox.

39. "SEC Settles with Aguirre," Government Accountability Project.

40. Susan Antilla, "Mary Jo White's Past and the Future of the SEC," *Bloomberg*,
     February 7, 2013, http://www.bloomberg.com/news/2013-02-07/mary-jo
     -white-s-past-and-the-future-of-the-sec.html.

41. Gary J. Aguirre, email exchange with author, December 22, 2012.

42. Ibid.

CHAPTER 10: POGO STICKS

1. Subcommittee on Senate Resolutions 84 and 234, The Pecora Committee,
    June 6, 1934, http://www.senate.gov/artandhistory/history/common/inves

tigations/Pecora.htm; Stock Exchange Practices: Report of the Committee on Banking and Currency, 73rd Congress, US Senate, June 6, 1934,
http://www.senate.gov/artandhistory/history/common/investigations/pdf
/Pecora_FinalReport.pdf.

2. Banking Act of 1933, Federal Reserve Bank of New York, Circular No. 1248,
    June 22, 1933, http://archive.org/stream/FullTextTheGlass-steagallActA
    .k.a.TheBankingActOf1933/1933_01248#page/n0/mode/1up/search/Fede
    ral+Deposit+Insurance+Corporation.

3. "The Financial Crisis Inquiry Report," Superintendent of Documents, *US
    Government Printing Office,* January 2011, http://www.gpo.gov/fdsys/pkg
    /GPO-FCIC/pdf/GPO-FCIC.pdf.

4. Statement of Sheila C. Bair, Chairman, Federal Deposit Insurance Corpo-
    ration on the Causes and Current State of the Financial Crisis before the
    Financial Crisis Inquiry Commission; Room 1100, Longworth House Of-
    fice Building, January 14, 2010, http://www.fdic.gov/news/news/speeches
    /chairman/spjan1410.html.

5. "The Financial Crisis Inquiry Report," Superintendent of Documents.

6. Ibid.

7. Ibid.

8. "Accounting Faculty Member Earns Awards for His Financial Crisis Cour-
    age," *Naveen Jindal School of Management Newsletter,* April 2012, http://
    jindal.utdallas.edu/newsletters/emanagement/april-2012/accounting
    -faculty-member-earns-awards-for-his-financial-crisis-courage/.

9. "Alliance for Economic Stability Urges Financial Crisis Inquiry Commission
    to Investigate FINRA," *PR Newswire,* April 12, 2010, http://www.prnews
    wire.com/news-releases/alliance-for-economic-stability-urges-financial
    -crisis-inquiry-commission-to-investigate-finra-90631079.html.

10. Statement by James K. Galbraith, Lloyd M. Bentsen, Jr. Chair in Govern-
    ment/Business Relations, Lyndon B. Johnson School of Public Affairs, The
    University of Texas at Austin, before the Subcommittee on Crime, Senate
    Judiciary Committee, May 4, 2010, http://utip.gov.utexas.edu/Flyers/Gal
    braithMay4SubCommCrimeRV.pdf.

11. Ibid.

12. Letter to Congress calling for Increased Oversight of Financial Self-
    Regulators, Project on Government Oversight, February 23, 2010, http://
    www.pogo.org/our-work/letters/2010/er-fra-20100223-2.html.

13. Ibid.

14. Ibid.

CHAPTER 11: TOO BIG TO REGULATE

1. Michael J. Moore and Christine Harper, "Goldman Sachs Demands Col-
    lateral It Won't Dish Out," *Bloomberg,* March 15, 2010, http://www.bloom
    berg.com/apps/news?pid=newsarchive&sid=af6uIAFTSorY&pos=10.

2. Pat Garofalo, "11 Facts You Need to Know About the Nation's Big-
    gest Banks," *Think Progress,* October 7, 2011, http://thinkprogress.org
    /economy/2011/10/07/338887/1-facts-biggest-banks.

3. Peter Cohan, "Big Risk: $1.2 Quadrillion Derivatives Market Dwarfs
    World GDP," *Daily Finance,* June 9, 2010, http://www.dailyfinance
    .com/2010/06/09/risk-quadrillion-derivatives-market-gdp/.

4. Dodd-Frank Wall Street Reform and Consumer Protection Act, 111th Congress of the United States of America, January 5, 2010, http://www.sec.gov /about/laws/wallstreetreform-cpa.pdf.

5. "U.S. Capital Markets Competitiveness: The Unfinished Agenda," *Center for Capital Markets Competetiveness*, July 19, 2011, http://www.uschamber .com/sites/default/files/reports/1107_UnfinishedAgenda_WEB.pdf.

6. Victoria McGrane and Jon Hilsenrath, "Fed Writes Sweeping Rules from Behind Closed Doors," *Wall Street Journal*, February 21, 2012, http:// online.wsj.com/article/SB100014240529702040598045772251228924503 12.html.

7. "Big Banks Dominate Dodd-Frank Meetings with Regulators," *Sunlight Foundation*, July 19, 2012, http://sunlightfoundation.com/blog/2012/07/19 /dodd-frank-two-years-later/.

8. "One Year Later: The Consequences of the Dodd-Frank Act," The Financial Services Committee, accessed September 4, 2013, http://financialservices .house.gov/uploadedfiles/financialservices-doddfrank-report.pdf.

9. Dunstan Prial, "SEC Says New Financial Regulation Law Exempts It from Public Disclosure," *Fox Business*, July 28, 2010, http://www.foxbusiness.com /markets/2010/07/28/sec-says-new-finreg-law-exempts-public-disclosure/.

10. "SEC Withholds Records on Oversight of Regulatory Group," Project on Government Oversight, June 16, 2011, http://pogoblog.typepad.com /pogo/2011/06/sec-withholds-records-on-oversight-of-self-regulatory -group.html.

11. *David P. Weber vs. United States Securities and Exchange Commission and Mary L. Schapiro*, United States District Court for the District of Columbia, November 15, 2012, http://www.senseoncents.com/wp-content/up loads/2012/11/Weber_complaint.pdf.

12. Cary J. Hansel, "SEC Settles Whistleblowers Lawsuit Agrees to Clear David P. Weber's Record Makes $580,000 Whistleblower Retaliation Payment," *Joseph, Greenwald & Laake, P.A.*, June 10, 2013, http://www.senseoncents .com/wp-content/uploads/2013/06/Weber_Settlement_Press_Release.pdf.

13. "The First Five Years: FINRA'S TOP 25 ENFORCEMENT CASES," *Securities Technology Monitor*, accessed September 4, 2013, http://www .securitiestechnologymonitor.com/gallery/finra-first-five-years-25-top -cases-31057-1.html.

14. Ibid.

15. "Securities Regulation: Opportunities Exist to Improve SEC's Oversight of the Financial Industry Regulatory Authority," US Government Accountability Office, May 2012, http://www.gao.gov/assets/600/591222.pdf.

16. William Alden, "Khuzami's New Job," *Dealb%k, The New York Times*, July 23, 2013, http://dealbook.nytimes.com/2013/07/23/morning-agenda -khuzamis-new-job/?_r=0.

17. "U.S. Capital Markets Competitiveness: The Unfinished Agenda," *Center for Capital Markets Competitiveness*, July 19, 2011, www.uschamber.com/sites /default/files/reports/1107_UnfinishedAgenda_WEB.pdf.

CHAPTER 12: CHANGING THE SHEETS

1. *The Declaration of Independence*, http://www.archives.gov/exhibits/charters /declaration_transcript.html

2. Jon Hilsenrath, "How a Trust Deficit Is Hurting the Economy," *Wall Street Journal,* January 27, 2013, http://online.wsj.com/article/SB1000142412788 7323854904578264161278400462.html.

3. "The Rule of Law Index," *World Justice Project,* accessed September 11, 2013, http://www.worldjusticeproject.org/rule-of-law-index/.

4. Vito J. Racanelli, "Is America Becoming an Anti-Risk Welfare State?" *Barron's,* April 28, 2012, http://online.barrons.com/article/SB5000142405311 190359150457736193244277236.html#articleTabs_article%3D1.

5. Ibid.

6. Commissioner Luis A. Aguilar, "Outmanned and Outgunned: Fighting on Behalf of Investors Despite Efforts to Weaken Investor Protections," *U.S. Securities and Exchange Commission,* April 16, 2013, http://www.sec.gov /news/speech/2013/spch041613laa.htm.

7. Sheila Bair, *Bull By The Horns: Fighting to Save Main Street from Wall Street and Wall Street from Itself,* New York, NY: Free Press, 2012, 338.

8. Commissioner Luis A. Aguilar.

9. Susanna Kim Ripken, "Corporate First Amendment Rights After Citizens United: An Analysis of the Popular Movement to End the Constitutional Personhood of Corporations," *University of Pennsylvania Journal of Business Law,* Volume 14:1, 209-259, accessed September 4, 2013, https://www.law .upenn.edu/live/files/158-ripken14upajbusl2092011pdf.

10. Lawrence Lessig, "How Money Corrupts Congress and a Plan to Stop It," *Long Now Foundation,* January 17, 2012, http://longnow.org /seminars/02012/jan/17/how-money-corrupts-congress-and-plan-stop-it/.

11. "Final Report," *High-level Expert Group on reforming the structure of the EU banking sector,* October 2, 2012, accessed September 27, 2013, http:// ec.europa.eu/internal_market/bank/docs/high-level_expert_group/report _en.pdf.

INDEX